INTRODUCTION TO DBMS: THEORY & PRACTICALS

AUTHOR

Dr. Myneni Madhu Bala

Professor, Department of Computer Science Engineering,
Institute of Aeronautical Engineering,
Medchal, Malkajgiri-500043, Telangana

REVIEWER

Dr. Sanjiva Shankar Dubey

Professor, Birla Institute of Management Technology,
Greater Noida, Gautam Buddha Nagar-201306, Uttar Pradesh

KHANNA BOOK PUBLISHING CO. (P) Ltd.
4C/4344, Ansari Road, Darya Ganj,
New Delhi, India

All India Council for Technical Education
Nelson Mandela Marg, Vasant Kunj,
New Delhi, India

ISBN: 978-93-5538-865-0

Book Code: DIP461EN

Introduction To DBMS: Theory and Practicals

by Dr. Myneri Madhu Bala

First Edition: 2026

Originally Published by:

All India Council for Technical Education, Ministry of Education, GOI

Exclusively Published & Distributed by:

Khanna Book Publishing Co. (P) Ltd.

4C/4344, Ansari Road, Daryaganj,
New Delhi (INDIA)

Visit us at: **www.khannabooks.com**

Write us at: **contact@khannabooks.com**

To view complete list of books, Please scan the QR Code: KPH

Printed in Bharat.

प्रो. म. जगदीश कुमार
अध्यक्ष
Prof. M. Jagadesh Kumar
Chairman

सत्यमेव जयते

आज़ादी का अमृत महोत्सव

अखिल भारतीय तकनीकी शिक्षा परिषद्
(भारत सरकार का एक सांविधिक निकाय)
(शिक्षा मंत्रालय, भारत सरकार)
नेल्सन मंडेला मार्ग, वसंत कुंज, नई दिल्ली–110070
दूरभाष : 011–26131498
ई–मेल : chairman@aicte-india.org

ALL INDIA COUNCIL FOR TECHNICAL EDUCATION
(A STATUTORY BODY OF THE GOVT. OF INDIA)
(Ministry of Education, Govt. of India)
Nelson Mandela Marg, Vasant Kunj, New Delhi-110070
Phone : 011-26131498
E-mail : chairman@aicte-india.org

FOREWORD

Engineers are the backbone of the modern society. It is through them that engineering marvels have happened and improved quality of life across the world. They have driven humanity towards greater heights in a more evolved and unprecedented manner.

The All India Council for Technical Education (AICTE), led from the front and assisted students, faculty & institutions in every possible manner towards the strengthening of the technical education in the country. AICTE is always working towards promoting quality Technical Education to make India a modern developed nation with the integration of modern knowledge & traditional knowledge for the welfare of mankind.

An array of initiatives have been taken by AICTE in last decade which have been accelerate now by the National Education Policy (NEP) 2020. The implementation of NEP under the visionary leadership of Hon'ble Prime Minister of India envisages the provision for education in regional languages to all, thereby ensuring that every graduate becomes competent enough and is in a position to contribute towards the national growth and development through innovation & entrepreneurship.

One of the spheres where AICTE had been relentlessly working since 2021-22 is providing high quality books prepared and translated by eminent educators in various Indian languages to its engineering students at Under Graduate & Diploma level. For the second year students, AICTE has identified 87 books at Under Graduate and Diploma Level courses, for translation in 12 Indian languages - Hindi, Tamil, Gujarati, Odia, Bengali, Kannada, Urdu, Punjabi, Telugu, Marathi, Assamese & Malayalam. In addition to the English medium, the 1044 books in different Indian Languages are going to support to engineering students to learn in their mother tongue. Currently, there are 39 institutions in 11 states offering courses in Indian languages in 7 disciplines like Biomedical Engineering, Civil Engineering, Computer Science & Engineering, Electrical Engineering, Electronics & Communication Engineering, Information Technology Engineering & Mechanical Engineering, Architecture, and Interior Designing. This will become possible due to active involvement and support of universities/institutions in different states.

On behalf of AICTE, I express sincere gratitude to all distinguished authors, reviewers and translators from different IITs, NITs and other institutions for their admirable contribution in a very short span of time.

AICTE is confident that these out comes based books with their rich content will help technical students master the subjects with factor comprehension and greater ease.

(Prof. M. Jagadesh Kumar)

ACKNOWLEDGEMENT

The authors are grateful to the authorities of AICTE, particularly Prof. M. Jagadesh Kumar, Chairman; Prof. M. P. Poonia, Vice-Chairman; Prof. Rajive Kumar, Member-Secretary and Dr. Amit Kumar Srivastava, Director, Faculty Development Cell for their planning to publish the books on Introductions to DBMS: Theory & Practicals. We sincerely acknowledge the valuable contributions of the reviewer of the book Dr. Sanjiva Shankar Dubey, Professor, Birla Institute of Management Technology for making it students' friendly and giving a better shape in an artistic manner.

This book is an outcome of various suggestions of AICTE members, experts and authors who shared their opinion and thought to further develop the engineering education in our country. Acknowledgements are due to the contributors and different workers in this field whose published books, review articles, papers, photographs, footnotes, references and other valuable information enriched us at the time of writing the book.

Myneni Madhu Bala

PREFACE

The book titled "Introduction to DBMS: Theory and Practicals" is an outcome of the rich experience of our teaching of computer science courses. The initiation of writing this book is to expose database systems to the computer science students, the fundamentals of dababase systems as well as enable them to get an insight of the subject. Keeping in mind the purpose of wide coverage as well as to provide essential supplementary information, we have included the topics recommended by AICTE, in a very systematic and orderly manner throughout the book. Efforts have been made to explain the fundamental concepts of the subject in the simplest possible way.

During the process of preparation of the manuscript, we have considered the various standard text books and accordingly we have developed sections like numerical problems, case studies with solutions and practical sections etc. While preparing the different sections emphasis has also been laid on definitions, syntaxes and semantics and also on comprehensive synopsis of syntaxes and semantics and algorithms for a quick revision of the core concepts. The book covers all types of medium and advanced level problems/case studies and these have been presented in a very logical and systematic manner. The stages of those case studies have been tested over many years of teaching to a wide variety of students.

Apart from illustrations and examples as required, we have enriched the book with solved case studies in every unit for proper understanding of the related topics. It is important to note that in each unit, we have included the relevant laboratory practical. In addition, besides some essential information for the users under the heading "Know More" we have clarified some essential basic information in the appendix and annexure section.

As far as the present book is concerned, "Introduction to DBMS: Theory & Practicals" is meant to provide a thorough grounding in database systems on the topics covered. This part of the computer science book will prepare diploma students to apply the knowledge of database systems to tackle 21st century and onward engineering challenges and address the related stimulated questions. The subject matters are presented in a constructive manner so that an computer science diploma prepares students to work in different sectors or in national laboratories at the very forefront of technology.

We sincerely hope that the book will inspire the students to learn and discuss the ideas behind basic principles of relational database management systems and will surely contribute to the development of a solid foundation of the subject. We would be thankful to all beneficial comments and suggestions which will contribute to the improvement of the future editions of the book. It gives us immense pleasure to place this book in the hands of the teachers and students. It was indeed a big pleasure to work on different aspects covering in the book.

Myneni Madhu Bala

OUTCOME BASED EDUCATION

For the implementation of an outcome based education the first requirement is to develop an outcome based curriculum and incorporate an outcome based assessment in the education system. By going through outcome based assessments, evaluators will be able to evaluate whether the students have achieved the outlined standard, specific and measurable outcomes. With the proper incorporation of outcome based education there will be a definite commitment to achieve a minimum standard for all learners without giving up at any level. At the end of the programme running with the aid of outcome based education, a student will be able to arrive at the following outcomes:

Programme Outcomes (POs) are statements that describe what students are expected to know and be able to do upon graduating from the program. These relate to the skills, knowledge, analytical ability attitude and behaviour that students acquire through the program. The POs essentially indicate what the students can do from subject-wise knowledge acquired by them during the program. As such, POs define the professional profile of an engineering diploma graduate.

National Board of Accreditation (NBA) has defined the following seven POs for an Engineering diploma graduate:

PO1. Basic and Discipline specific knowledge: Apply knowledge of basic mathematics, science and engineering fundamentals and engineering specialization to solve the engineering problems.

PO2. Problem analysis: Identify and analyses well-defined engineering problems using codified standard methods.

PO3. Design/ development of solutions: Design solutions for well-defined technical problems and assist with the design of systems components or processes to meet specified needs.

PO4. Engineering Tools, Experimentation and Testing: Apply modern engineering tools and appropriate technique to conduct standard tests and measurements.

PO5. Engineering practices for society, sustainability and environment: Apply appropriate technology in context of society, sustainability, environment and ethical practices.

PO6. Project Management: Use engineering management principles individually, as a team member or a leader to manage projects and effectively communicate about well-defined engineering activities.

PO7. Life-long learning: Ability to analyse individual needs and engage in updating in the context of technological changes.

COURSE OUTCOMES

By the end of the course the students are expected to learn:

CO-1: How to design a database, database-based applications

CO-2: How to use a DBMS.

CO-3: The critical role of database system in designing several information system-based software systems or applications.

Mapping of Course Outcomes with Programme Outcomes to be done according to the matrix given below:

Course Outcomes	Expected Mapping with Programme Outcomes (1- Weak Correlation; 2- Medium correlation; 3- Strong Correlation)						
	PO-1	**PO-2**	**PO-3**	**PO-4**	**PO-5**	**PO-6**	**PO-7**
CO-1	3	3	3	3	1	1	3
CO-2	3	2	2	2	1	1	3
CO-3	3	3	3	3	1	1	3

GUIDELINES FOR TEACHERS

To implement Outcome Based Education (OBE) knowledge level and skill set of the students should be enhanced. Teachers should take a major responsibility for the proper implementation of OBE. Some of the responsibilities (not limited to) for the teachers in OBE system may be as follows:

- Within reasonable constraint, they should manipulate time to the best advantage of all students.
- They should assess the students only upon certain defined criterion without considering any other potential ineligibility to discriminate them.
- They should try to grow the learning abilities of the students to a certain level before they leave the institute.
- They should try to ensure that all the students are equipped with the quality knowledge as well as competence after they finish their education.
- They should always encourage the students to develop their ultimate performance capabilities.
- They should facilitate and encourage group work and team work to consolidate newer approach.
- They should follow Blooms taxonomy in every part of the assessment.

Bloom's Taxonomy

Level	Teacher should Check	Student should be able to	Possible Mode of Assessment
Creating	Students ability to create	Design or Create	Mini project
Evaluating	Students ability to Justify	Argue or Defend	Assignment
Analysing	Students ability to distinguish	Differentiate or Distinguish	Project/Lab Methodology
Applying	Students ability to use information	Operate or Demonstrate	Technical Presentation/ Demonstration
Understanding	Students ability to explain the ideas	Explain or Classify	Presentation/Seminar
Remembering	Students ability to recall (or remember)	Define or Recall	Quiz

GUIDELINES FOR STUDENTS

Students should take equal responsibility for implementing the OBE. Some of the responsibilities (not limited to) for the students in OBE system are as follows:

- Students should be well aware of each Unit Outcome (UO) before the start of a unit in each and every course.
- Students should be well aware of each Course Outcome (CO) before the start of the course.
- Students should be well aware of each Programme Outcome (PO) before the start of the programme.
- Students should think critically and reasonably with proper reflection and action.
- Learning of the students should be connected and integrated with practical and real life consequences.
- Students should be well aware of their competency at every level of OBE.

ABBREVIATIONS AND SYMBOLS

List of Abbreviations

General Terms			
Abbreviations	**Full form**	**Abbreviations**	**Full form**
DB	Database	SQL	Structured Query Language
DBMS	Database Management Systems	OODB	Object-Oriented Databases
DBA	Database Administrators	XML	Extensible Markup Language
ER	Entity-Relationship	EER	Enhanced Entity-Relationship
DML	Data Manipulation Language	TRC	Tuple Relational Calculus
DDL	Data Definition Language	DRC	Domain Relational Calculus
PC	Personal Computer	TCL	Transaction Control Language
ODBC	Open Database Connectivity	DCL	Data Control Language
JDBC	Java Database Connectivity	IC	Integrity Constraints
WWW	World Wide Web	FD	Functional Dependencies

List of Symbols

Symbols	Description
$\vee$	OR
$\wedge$	AND
$\neg$	NOT
$\exists$	there exists
$\forall$	for all
AXB	Cartesian-Product Operation
$\bowtie$	natural-join
σ Sigma	selection
Π Pi	Projection
–	difference
$\cup$	Union

LIST OF FIGURES

CONTENTS

1 INTRODUCTION

UNIT SPECIFICS

Through this unit we have discussed the following aspects:

- *Need and Importance of Database systems*
- *Example database system*
- *Database users*
- *Advantages of Database systems in real-time applications*
- *Evolutions of Database Applications*
- *Data Models, Data Schemas*
- *Data constructs, Instances, state of Database*
- *Database Architecture*
- *Database Languages*

The practical applications of the topics are discussed for generating further curiosity and creativity as well as to improve problem-solving capacity.

Besides giving a large number of multiple-choice questions as well as questions of short and long answer types marked in two categories following lower and higher order of Bloom's taxonomy, assignments through several numerical problems, a list of references, and suggested readings are given in the unit so that one can go through them for practice. It is important to note that for getting more information on various topics of interest some QR codes have been provided in different sections which can be scanned for relevant supportive knowledge.

After the related practical, based on the content, there is a "Know More" section. This section has been carefully designed so that the supplementary information provided in this part becomes beneficial for the users of the book. This section mainly highlights the initial activity, examples of some interesting facts, analogy, history of the development of the subject focusing on the salient observations and finding, timelines starting from the development of the concerned topics up to the recent time, applications of the subject matter for our day-to-day real life or/and industrial applications on a variety of aspects, case study related to environmental, sustainability, social and ethical issues whichever applicable, and finally inquisitiveness and curiosity topics of the unit.

RATIONALE

This Introduction unit on Database systems helps students to get a primary idea about the real-time database applications, needs, and importance of relational database systems. It explains the concepts, models, schemas, users, languages, and architectures of the database system. All these basic aspects are relevant to starting the database system implementation. It then explains clearly about database model, schema development, and architecture views. All these are discussed at length to develop the database systems. Some related case studies are pointed out with an extension to the data model and schema development, which can help further in getting a clear idea of the concern topics on database systems.

Databases are an important branch of computer science that essentially deals with information and data and their effect on information retrieval. Database systems started their journey by traditional data processing (file system) and storage and then explaining it in terms of relational database management. This permits one to analyze the operations of many day-to-day transactions around us. But at the same time, it covers the database interactions and interfaces of the web, XML, and cloud. Its practical applications are related to the model, construction, and operation of different types of database systems and tools.

PRE-REQUISITES

Mathematics: Calculus, Algebra (Class XII)
Computer Science: problem-solving with programming (Class XII)

UNIT OUTCOMES

The List of outcomes of this unit is as follows:

U1-O1: Relate the real-time systems with database systems

U1-O2: Realize the need and importance of database systems for storage, manipulation, and retrieval of data.

U1-O3: Summarize the architectural views of the database system

U1-O4: Interpret the database system with schemas

U1-O5: Develop a database model with schema and languages for real-time system

Unit-1 Outcomes	EXPECTED MAPPING WITH COURSE OUTCOMES (1- Weak Correlation; 2- Medium correlation; 3- Strong Correlation)					
	CO-1	CO-2	CO-3	CO-4	CO-5	CO-6
U1-O1	3	1	3	-	-	-
U1-O2	1	1	1	-	-	-
U1-O3	2	2	3	-	-	-
U1-O4	3	3	3	-	-	-
U1-O5	3	3	3	-	-	-

1.1. DATABASE FUNDAMENTALS

Database systems play a significant role in modern civilization. In general, most of our daily activities require interacting with a database system in some way. For example, a bank transaction involves either depositing or withdrawing money; online purchases of electronic goods like computers, laptops, toys, books, and mobile phones through e-commerce sites like Flipkart and Amazon, hotel, rail, bus, or airline bookings, and computerized library catalogue to look up a bibliographic item are all activities that require to access a database through a computer program or a person. The supermarket database that stores all inventory and sales transactions of grocery products are frequently and automatically updated. The rising usage of computers has a significant impact on databases and database technologies. Every sector that uses computers, including business, electronic commerce, engineering, medical, genetics, law, education, and library science, depends on it.

A database (DB) system is a collection of related data, which refers to well-known facts that may be noted down and have underlying significance.

Examples include the names, numbers, and addresses of the employees and students.

A computer system and programs like Microsoft Access or Excel are used to process and store this information on disk or an indexed address book.

The following implicit characteristics apply to databases:

- Logically unified collection of information with inherent meaning
- Represents part of the real-world
- Created, constructed, and filled with information with a specific goal in mind.

Along with the characteristics, it must have a target audience in mind as well as have user-facing applications.

1.1.1 NEED AND IMPORTANCE OF DATABASE SYSTEMS

The majority of the data saved and retrieved in traditional database systems is either textual or numerical, and it is stored in a typical file-processing system that is supported by a traditional operating system. The system uses flat files to hold permanent records, and separate application programs are required to write to and read from the proper files. Before the development of database management systems (DBMSs), organizations could only save information digitally.

Traditional databases and file processing's limitations:

Accessing data: Once a specific application software is created for a task. Other tasks cannot be done; they are not supported. For instance, the software is created to retrieve a list of all students. It does not support collecting a list of students who have successfully finished 22 credits. Because of this, traditional file processing environments do not efficiently or easily support all necessary data retrievals.

Storing redundant data: Data redundancy occurs when the same information appears several times in a typical file processing context. For instance, if a student majors major mathematics and botany, the address and phone number of such student may be found in a file that contains student records from both departments. Due to the redundancy, storage and access costs are increased. Additionally, it can result in inconsistent data. For instance, the records of another department may not reflect a change in a contact number made in one department.

Data Isolation: In a typical file processing environment, all relevant data is dispersed among numerous files in diverse formats. As a result, retrieving right data through application programs is challenging.

Integrity issues: In a standard file processing environment, it is challenging to change or add additional consistency restrictions to the application software that stores the data with them. When limitations contain several data items from various files, the issue is exacerbated.

Concurrent access: A faster response time and allowing numerous users to update the data at once are key to the system's overall performance. In a file processing context, it is not feasible.

1.1.2. DATA VIEW

A relational database is made up of a group of connected data items and several that let users access and edit the data. A database system's goal is to give users an abstract view of the data. In other words, the system hides some information about the data's maintenance and storage.

Data Abstraction?

In real-time, the usability and popularity of a software system rely on the effective retrieval of data. In all ways, many users are not computer proficient. Therefore, to make users' interactions with the system simpler, developers hide the complexity from users at several levels of abstraction.

All the data is not required by all database users. Users must therefore only access a portion of the database. To make their engagement with the system simpler, there is a view level of abstraction. For the same database, the system might offer a variety of views. The link between the three levels of abstraction is depicted in Fig. 1.1. (Low to high).

Physical Level - How the data is physically stored.

Logical Level - What data and relationships among them are stored in the database? This is referred to as physical data independence. The Database administrators (DBA) will

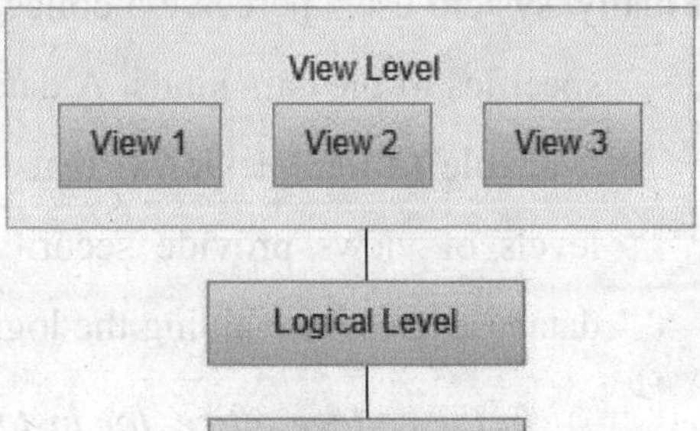

Fig. 1.1 Levels of Data View

decide what part of the information to store in the database with the logical level of abstraction.

View Level - describes a part of the entire database.

A college organization, for instance, might have fields:

- ✓ faculty records - faculty_ID, Faculty_name, dept_name, and salary_amt.
- ✓ department records - department_id, department_name, location, and budget_amt
- ✓ course records – course_id, course_title, department_name, and credit_score
- ✓ student records – student_ID, student_name, department_name, and total_credits

Physical Level:

Faculty, department, course, and student records can be thought of as a block of successive storage spaces on a physical level. Database administrators are concerned with the particulars of data stored physically.

Logical Level:

Each record's type description and how these record types relate to one another are explained at the logical level. At this level of abstraction, programming languages are used by database managers and programmers.

Finally, system users perceive a collection of applications at the view level that hides the specifics of the data kinds. A database user can view exactly required or everything available (different views) that have been defined for the database. The different levels of views provide security by restricting users from specific areas of the database access by hiding the logical level of the information.

In the college office, for instance, assistants can view students (a portion of the database), but they are restricted to access information regarding the salaries of faculty.

1.1.3 EXAMPLE DATABASE SYSTEM OF A COLLEGE

*An example system would be a **College database** that would be used to maintain information regarding major entities such as student, course, and grade in a college. Initially, the database is set up with five files having identical data records.*

STUDENT file contains information about each student;

COURSE file contains information about each course;

SECTION file contains information about all sections of a course;

GRADEREPORT file contains information about student grades received in different completed sections;

PRE REQUISITE file contains information about each course's prerequisites

STEP 1:

In order to define this database, we must describe the data items that will be kept in each record's structure shown in figure 1.2.

***STUDENT** data contains information about the Roll_ number, student_ Name, Class (like Firstyear / "1", Secondyear / "2"), Major course("Mathematics" / "MATH" and "Computer Science" / "CS").*

***COURSE** data contains information about the course_ name, number of credits, offered department.*

For every data element contained within a record, a data type must also be specified.

***GRADE** REPORT data contains a Grade (a single character in the given set {"A," "B," "C," "D," "F," and "I,"} and name of student is a string (having alphabetic characters), Roll number is an integer.*

The values of a data item may alternatively be represented via a coding scheme.

The Class of a STUDENT (such as 1, 2, 3, 4, and 5 for freshmen, sophomore, junior, senior, and graduate student, respectively.

We keep information in the relevant file to denote as student details, course details, section, grade details, and pre requisites as a record in order to build the college database. It should be noted that records in different files might be connected.

For instance, (in figure 1.2), in the GRADE REPORT file two records details are filled with amit grades in one section are tied to the record for amit in the STUDENT file.

In the PREREQUISITE file, each entry is linked with two course records, one for the course itself and the other for the prerequisite.

Student_Details			
Student_Roll No	**Student Name**	**Class**	**Major**
20951A0506	Amit	2	CS
21951A0536	Singh	1	CS

Course_Details			
Course Code	**Course Name**	**Credit**	**Offered Department**
CS0101	Computer Programming	3	CS
MATH0103	Discrete Mathematics	4	MATH
CS0103	Introduction to Databases: Theory and Practical	3	CS
CS0102	Computer Networks	3	CS

Course_Prerequisite	
Course Code	**Prerequisite Code**
CS0103	CS0101
CS0330	MATH0103
CS0321	CS0101
CS0103	CS0102

Section_Details				
Section_No	**Course Code**	**Semester**	**Year**	**Faculty_Name**
8	CS0321	Even	18	Patel
7	CS0101	Odd	21	Roy
5	CS0102	Even	13	Singh

Grade_Report		
Student_Roll No	**Section_No**	**Grade**
20951A0506	5	A
21951A0536	2	B
18951A0589	23	A
16991A0519	2	C

Fig. 1.2. A sample database data of a college application

Task:

Querying and updating are two aspects of database manipulation. The following are some examples of queries:

→ *Get "Amit's" transcript, which contains a list of all of his or her courses and grades.*

→ *List the prerequisites for the "Database" course;*

→ *Display the student names, who acquired the section of the course given in even 2020 and their grades;*

→ *Provide examples of changes, such as the following:*
Create a new segment of the "Database" with a courses for this semester. Change "Amit" class to sophomores. Enter "Amit" grade of "A" in the "Database" section from previous sem.

1.1.4. DATABASE DESIGN

There are three stages to the database design process Conceptual, Logical, and Physical. The requirement specification and analysis phase is the first step in designing a new application for both an existing database and a brand-new database. To make it simple to maintain, modify, and convert into a database implementation, these specifications are recorded and turned into a conceptual design that can be represented and edited using computerized tools. A Logical design of a system to be represented is done through a commercial DBMS.

1.1.5. DATABASE SYSTEM EVOLUTION

Over time, methods for processing and storing data have changed. In the beginning, greater emphasis was placed on data storage methods, such as relational databases in decentralized contexts and files on tapes and discs. Over time, data processing has progressed beyond payroll management to data analysis. Fig. 1.3 depicts the development of database systems from 1960 to 2000.

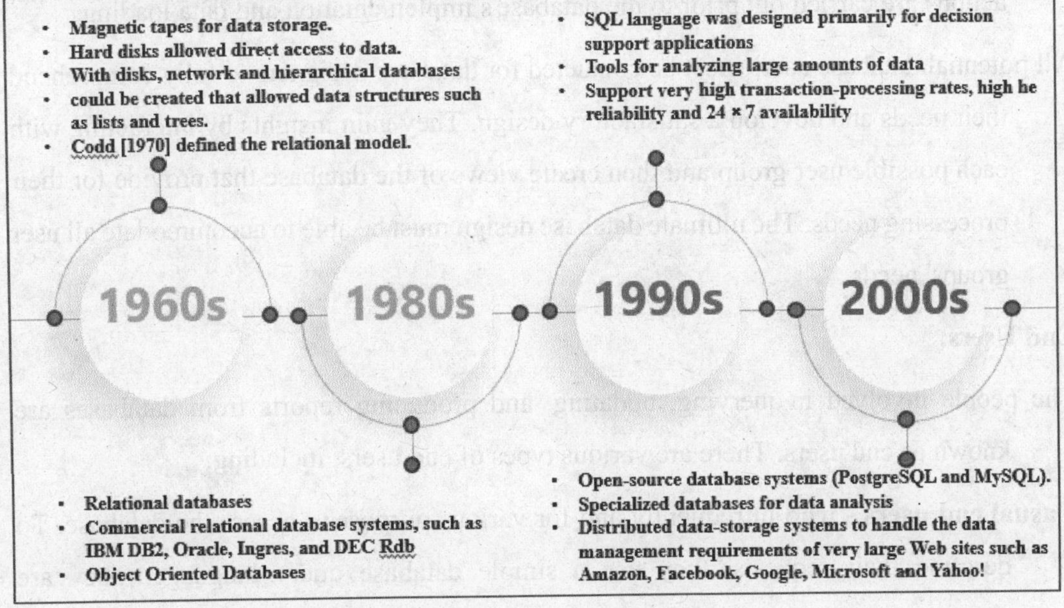

Fig. 1.3. History of Database systems

1.1.6. USERS OF DATABASES

A huge database with hundreds of users is designed, used, and maintained by numerous people in large organizations.

Administrators of databases

The Database Administrator (DBA) is the authority of granting users access to the database, organizing and controlling how it is used, and organizing necessary hardware and software resources. Security lapses and slow system responses are a few of the issues handled by the DBA.

Designers of Database

The database designers are responsible to determine the data that will be stored in the database and selecting the best structures for representing and store. Utmost all these actions are carried out prior to the database's implementation and data loading.

All potential database users must be contacted for database designers to fully comprehend their needs and develop a satisfactory design. They gain insights by interacting with each possible user group and then create views of the database that provide for their processing needs. The ultimate database design must be able to accommodate all user groups' needs.

End Users:

The people involved in querying, updating, and producing reports from databases are known as end users. There are various types of end users, including:

Casual end users - who infrequently and for various purposes - access the database. To describe their requests, they use a simple database query language. They are supervisors at medium or high levels or other infrequent browsers.

Naïve/parametric Users - Their primary duty is to continuously update and query the database using pre-programmed, thoroughly tested transactions, which are common.

These users carry out a variety of tasks:

1. Account balances are checked by bank tellers, who also post deposits and withdrawals.

2. Airlines, hotels, and car rental agencies all have reservation agents who can check availability and book bookings.

To update a database with all received parcels, workers at receiving stations for shipping businesses.

3. Engineers, scientists, business analysts, and other professionals with in-depth knowledge of the DBMS's features are examples of sophisticated end users.

Independent users - manage their databases by utilizing pre-built software packages that offer simple menus or graphics-based user interfaces.

An illustration would be a user of a tax preparation program who keeps a variety of personal financial information for program purposes.

Analysts and developers (Software Engineers)

They will identify the needs of users, particularly simple and parametric users to create specifications for pre-packaged standard transactions that fullfil these requirements. Application programmers convert these specifications into working programs, which they subsequently test, debug, record, and maintain. To effectively carry out their duties, these analysts and programmers—often referred to as software developers or software engineers—should be knowledgeable about the full scope of DBMS capabilities.

Designers and implementers of DBMS systems

They are concerned with creating a software package that includes the DBMS modules and interfaces. It is composed of several parts, or modules, such as those that implement the catalog, process query languages, process user interfaces, access, and buffer data, manage concurrency, handle data recovery, and handle security.

Tool Developers:

The tool developers will create packages to simplify database modelling and design, and for enhancing performance.

Operators and maintenance personnel:

The responsibility of operators and maintenance employees (system administration personnel) is the effective functioning of the database system and maintenance of the environment including hardware and software.

1.2. CONCEPTS OF A DATABASE

The essential terminology of database systems includes; schemas, instances, models.

1.2.1. A DATA MODEL AND SCHEMA

A data model is a collection of interrelated concepts that are used to define the database structure. It includes the related data type, relationship, and required constraints. It provides data abstraction to access different levels of users at their chosen level.

Data Model Categories

The data models have been categorized according to the types of concepts used:

1. Conceptual / High Level
2. Physical / Low Level
3. Representational / implementation

1. Conceptual / High Level

All high-level concepts (users recognized data) are named as an 'entity', 'attribute', and 'relationship'.

Entity - A concept or object is taken from the real world

Eg. an employee, a student in the database

Attribute – The specific characteristic of an entity

Eg. Employee_name, gross_salary are attributes of an employee

Relationship - an association between the existing entities

Eg. a relationship existed between an employee and a department can be defined as ***works-for***

An Entity-Relationship (ER) diagram illustrates the high-level conceptual data model.

2. Physical / Low Level

The low-level representation of data on physical storage (Eg. Magnetic disks) includes the files related to record format, ordering, and access details.

Eg. Indexing (Index term or keyword) used to access data

3. Implementation / Representational

The concepts are represented in an easily understandable way and hide storage details of the disk for end users. It is a commonly used model in commercial database management systems. The representational DB models are relational, legacy models like hierarchical and network.

Schema:

The Schema is the representation of a database system, is stated throughout database design, and is not expected to change repeatedly. A schema diagram will illustrate the description of the database. Fig. 1.4 illustrate the database schema of student details.

Student_Details

Student_Roll No	Student Name	Branch	Major	Section

Course_Details

Course Code	Course Name	Credit	Offered Department

Course_Prerequisite

Course Code	Prerequisite Code

Section_Details

Section_No	Course Code	Semester	Year	Faculty_Name

Grade_Report

Student_Roll No	Section_No	Grade

Fig. 1. 4. Illustration of Student Schema Diagram

1.2.2. INSTANCES, SCHEMA CONSTRUCTS, STATE OF DATABASE

Instances:

The instances are present sets of incidents in the database, also termed the state of a database or snapshot.

Shema Construct:

In any given state of the database, each schema construct is represented as a set of related instances.

The Student_details schema construct is represented with a set of student records as instances.

State of Database:

A database update with an insert, delete or change in data value in a record alters the state of a database. It does not affect the database schema. In general, several database states are raised to a specific database schema. The database states are listed as Initial, Empty, Current, and Valid. Fig. 1.5 illustrates the various database states and descriptions.

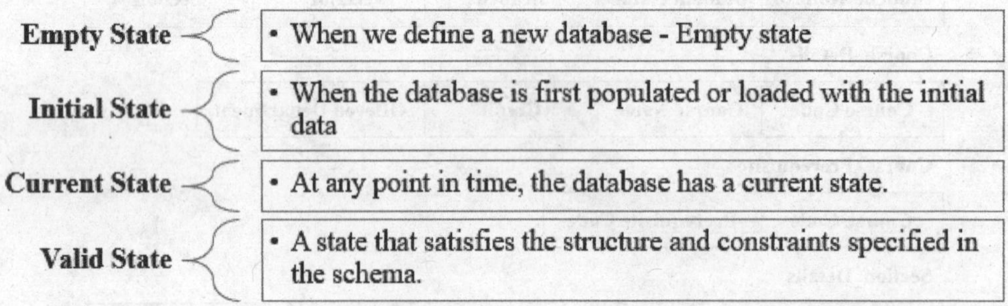

Fig. 1.5. Database states

1.3. ARCHITECTURE

The database architecture captures the many essential functional modules of a DB system along with the associations existed between them. The database architecture comprises essential components as illustrated in Fig. 1.6. It is significantly inclined by the computer system with the database system. The database system comprises of majorly two functional components:

1. Storage Manager
2. Query Processor

Each component is again accommodated with multiple database tables. And multiple types of users are connected through respective interfaces to the database system.

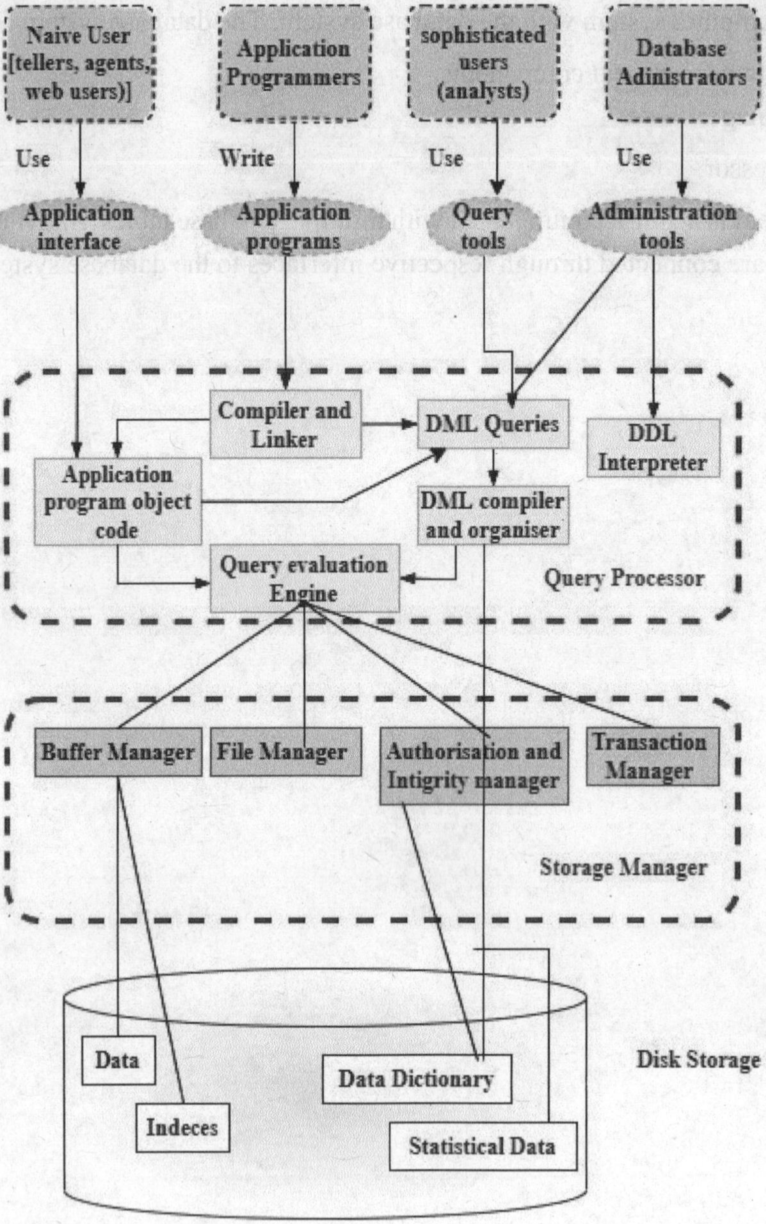

Fig. 1.6. Database Architecture

1.3.1. STORAGE AND QUERYING OF DATA

> **Megabyte** - 1024 Kilobytes or 1,048,576 Bytes
>
> **Gigabyte** - 1000 megabytes (in fact 1024) (1 billion bytes), and
>
> **Terabyte** - 1 million megabytes or (1 trillion bytes).

Disk storage: The database size is covered from gigabytes to terabytes. The main memory of computer systems cannot store ample information; disk is used as alternate storage. In query processing, the data moves between disk and main memory based on the requirement. This movement leads to slow processing. Hence, a system must minimize the need to move data between disk and main memory.

Few Physical data structures (files) maintained in the disk are:

1. Data Files – stores the actual data items of the database.
2. Data Dictionary – maintains the metadata (i.e. the structure of the database).
3. Indices – all index terms are stored; it is used to fast access data items.

Eg. Find the faculty data- with a specific faculty_ID, or all faculty_IDs.

The above tasks are completed by using an index of ID. Hashing technique is an alternative to indexing; It is faster in few cases but not in all cases.

4. Statistical Data – All statistical parameters of the data, used by the query processor to execute the query efficiently.

Storage Manager:

The storage manager acts as an interface in the middle of the disk storage (for low-level data) and the application programs or queries submitted to the system. It holds the accountability of interaction with the file manager; stores the raw data on the disk in the file system of operating systems; translates the DML statements into file system instructions. Therefore, the storage manager is accountable for the storage, retrieval, and updates of data in the database.

The storage manager comprises of:

1. Authorization and integrity manager ensures the constraints of data integrity and the access details of the authorized users.
2. Transaction manager ensures the database maintains in a consistent (correct) state in the aspect of system failures, and concurrent transactions without raising conflicts.
3. File manager is accountable for the distribution of disk space and appropriate data structure used to store on disk.
4. Buffer manager is accountable for fetching data from disk into main memory, and allocation to cache memory.

Query Processor:

The query processor translates the Data Manipulation Language(DML) and Data Definition Language(DDL) commands into a set of activities at the physical level of the database. The components include:

1. DDL interpreter – It interprets DDL commands and results from records are stored in the data dictionary.
2. DML compiler – It translates DML commands into low-level instructions which are understood by query evaluation engine.

Usually, a query is translated into no. of substitute evaluation procedures. It performs query optimization (i.e, the cost-effective evaluation among the changes).

3. Query evaluation engine – executes the DML compiler-generated low-level instructions.
4. DDL Interpreter – interprets the DDL Statements and recorded them as metadata.

1.3.2. DATABASE ARCHITECTURES

Database systems can be implemented in two ways centralized, another way as client/server.

The centralized architecture contains all hardware and software components (Application programs, user interface programs, database software, and compilers) which are available in one system (mainframe system) to process all functionalities of the database, applications programs, and user interface functionalities. Fig. 1.7 illustrates the components in a centralized architecture.

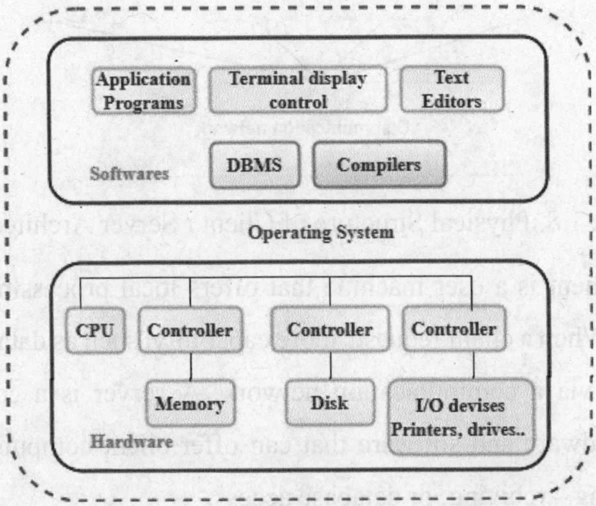

Fig. 1.7. Centralized Architecture

Client/server architectures emerged as DBMS systems gradually began to take advantage of the user side's computing capability. Most database system users often connect to it over a network rather than being physically present at the database system's location. So it's necessary to distinguish between client and server computers. Server machines run database systems, while client machines are utilized for remote work. A physical client/server architecture diagram is shown in Fig. 1.8. There are essentially three physical structure scenarios; computers that would only be client sites (for instance, workstations or PCs without discs or workstations or PCs with discs that only have client software installed), workstations would function as both clients and servers, workstations as dedicated servers.

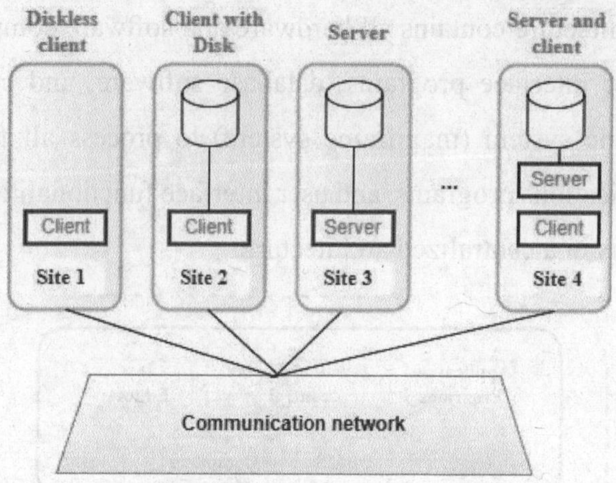

Fig. 1.8. Physical Structure of Client / Server Architecture

In this system, a client is a user machine that offers local processing and user interface capabilities. When a client requests more capability, such as database access, a server is connected via a communication network. A server is a computer system that combines hardware and software that can offer client computers services like file access, printing, archiving, or database access.

Applications for databases are usually divided into two or three components.

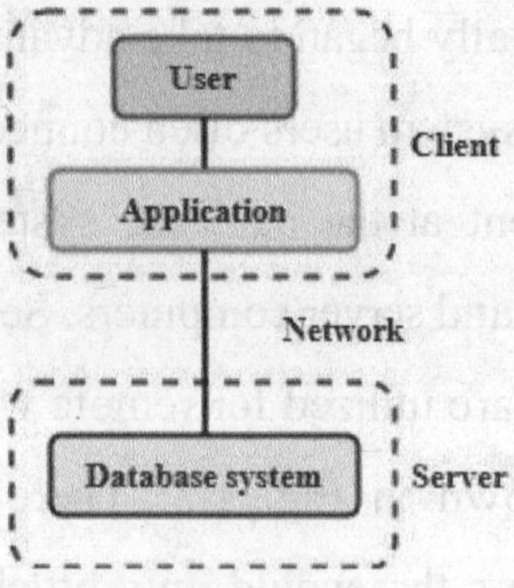

Fig. 1.9. A 2-tier Architecture

In a 2-tier paradigm, the application is located on the client-side machine and uses query language statements to access database system capabilities on the server machine. For establishing communication between the client and server machines, application program interface standards like ODBC and JDBC are engaged. The structure of the 2-tier database is shown in Fig. 1.9.

The client machine serves as the front end and does not directly interface with the database in a three-tier architecture. Instead, to access data, the client end interacts with an application server, which it subsequently does with a database system. The application server contains the business logic (which actions to take and under what circumstances) for the application. A three-tier architecture in general is shown in Fig. 1.10. It fits web applications that operate on the World Wide Web (WWW).

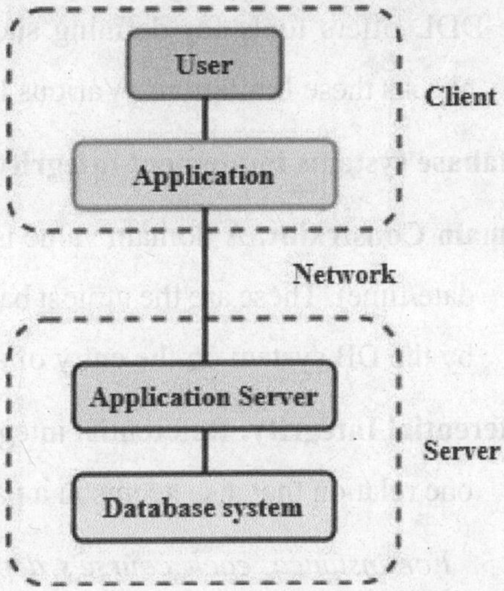

Fig. 1.10 A Three-tier Architecture

1.3.3. DATABASE LANGUAGES

Data definition language (DDL) is used to state the database schema and a data manipulation language (DML) is used to execute database queries and updates. In practice, the DDL and DML are not two separate languages; parts of a Structured Query Language (SQL). SQL is covered in detail in chapter 4.

Data Definition Language:

A DDL is used by DBA and database designers to define schemas and constraints to maintain consistency in the database. These are required only after one has done the initial phase of finalizing the data design and implementation of the database in the language of their choice.

Consider the scenario, where the college mandates that a department's account balance never go negative.

The DDL offers tools for defining such limitations. For every update, the DB system checks these limitations. Various limitations are discussed further.

Database systems implement integrity constraints:

Domain Constraint: A domain value is linked with all attributes (Eg., integer, character, date/time). These are the utmost basic form of integrity constraints. These are verified by the DB system on the entry of a new record.

Referential Integrity: Referential integrity refers to the assurance of a value appearing in one relation that also seems in a particular set of attributes in another relation.

For instance, each course's department name must be an existing object. More specifically, the deptname in the department table must match the deptname in the course record.

Assertions: The conditions that the database must satisfy *all the time*. The constraints such as Domain, and referential integrity are considered as special forms of assertions.

Eg., "Every department must have at least five courses offered in every semester" - articulated as an assertion.

Authorization: To implement data abstraction, the users are differentiated based on the diverse types of access they are permitted. These differentiations are expressed in terms of authorizations to the most common users such as read, insert, update and delete. The user access may assign all, none, or a combination of these types of authorization.

Authorizations:

Read - permits to read not modification of data

Insert - allows insertions of new records, but not modification of existing data

Update - allows modifications but not deletion of data

Data Manipulation Language:

Users need to have a method for modifying the database once the database schemas are put together and filled with data. Data retrieval, insertion, deletion, and modification are typical manipulations. For these uses, the DBMS offers a collection of operations or a language known as the data manipulation language (DML).

The data dictionary contains the metadata i.e, data about data - contains the result of the DDL. It is believed that the data dictionary is a unique kind of table that can only be read and modified by the database system itself (not a regular user). The data dictionary is consulted by the database system before reading or editing actual data.

1.4. ADVANTAGES OF DATABASE SYSTEMS IN REAL-TIME APPLICATIONS

Database applications are categorized according to real-time applications are:

1. Network and Hierarchical Systems
2. Fast response in relational databases
3. Object-oriented databases
4. XML databases

1.4.1. DATABASE APPLICATIONS WITH NETWORK AND HIERARCHICAL SYSTEMS

The combination of abstract relationships along with the physical storage and storing records on the disc was one of the key issues with early database systems. As a result, these systems lacked adequate capabilities for program-data independence and data abstraction. Early systems had the drawback of just offering programming language interfaces. Because new programs had to be built, tested, and debugged, adding additional queries and transactions became time-consuming and expensive.

Relational databases' ability to abstract data and increase application flexibility

With the motto of separation between the actual storage from its conceptual illustration and to establish a mathematical foundation for data representation and querying, relational databases were first proposed. High-level query languages with programming language interfaces were also made available by the relational data architecture allowing significantly faster creation of new queries.

As with past systems, initially, relational database systems were designed for the same applications and offered the flexibility to create new queries rapidly and rearrange the database as needs evolved. In comparison to preceding systems, data abstraction and program-data independence were therefore greatly enhanced. New indexing and stored methods helped boost performance and enhance query processing and optimization.

Object-Oriented Applications development with OODB

The development of OOP languages (the1980s) with the essentiality for storing and sharing complex and structured objects directed the growth of OODBs (object-oriented databases).

E-Commerce Applications with Exchange of Data on the Web Using XML

Due to the raise in E-Commerce application uses, web documents with HTML are massively created and required to store on web servers for other clients' access through hyperlinks. The XML is used for interchanging data among various DBs and web pages.

UNIT SUMMARY

- A database management system(DBMS) is a collection of all interconnected files and programs.

  Traditional file processing limitations:
  - Not efficient data Access
  - Redundant data storage
  - Data isolation
  - Data integrity
  - Concurrent access

- Data Abstraction is provided in three levels
  - Physical level
  - Logical Level
  - View Level

- Database Design process is implemented in three phases
  - Conceptual
  - Logical and
  - Physical

- Database users are categorised as
  - Administrators
  - Designers
  - End Users (Casual end user, Naïve end user)
  - System analysts and developers
  - Designers and implementers of DBMS
  - Tool developers
  - Operational and maintenance personal
- Database Applications with
  - Network and Hierarchical systems
  - Relational databases
  - OO applications with OODB
  - E-commerce applications with XML

- A data model is a gathering of interrelated concepts, used to define the structure of a database. The structure includes the related data type, relationship, and the required constraints. It provides data abstraction to access different levels of users at their chosen level.

- Data model categories are
    - Conceptual / High Level
    - Physical / Low Level
    - Representational / implementation

- The Schema is the depiction of a database system, is specified throughout database design and not likely to change repeatedly.
- The instances are present set of incidents in the database, also termed as state of a database or snapshot.
- A database update with an insert, delete or change of a data item in a record makes a change in state of a database.
- The database system comprises of majorly two functional components:
  1. Storage Manager(SM)
  2. Query Processor(QP)
- The storage manager acts as an interface between the disk storage (low level data) and the application programs or queries submitted to the system.
- The query processor translates the DML commands into set of actions at the physical level of database.
- Database systems can be implemented in two ways as centralized, or client/server, where one server and multiple client machines
- A data definition language (DDL) is used to specify the database schema and a data manipulation language (DML) is used to execute database queries and updates.
- In practice, the DDL and DML are not two separate languages; parts of a Structured Query Language (SQL).

EXERCISES

Multiple Choice Questions

1 DML stands for
 a. Data Manipulation language
 b. Dependency maintenance link
 c. Data Mining language
 d. Data maintenance language
2 In database management systems (DBMS) usage, the part to understand is
 a. Row
 b. Record
 c. Database
 d. File
3 Categories of models in DBMS are
 a. Object-based and Record-based
 b. Object-based and Field-based
 c. Object-based and Bit-based
 d. Object-based and Table-based
4 The collection of fields is called
 a. Fields
 b. Records
 c. Database
 d. File Based
5 Which one is not a component of a relational database?
 a. Entity
 b. Attribute
 c. Table
 d. Hierarchy
6 To use DBMS, the important one to understand is
 a. The physical schema
 b. All substances that the system supports
 c. One sub schema
 d. Both (A) and (B)
7 The group of data items for storage is termed as
 a. Record
 b. Title
 c. List
 d. String
8 User authorization is the responsibility of the
 a. Database administrator
 b. Database Manager
 c. Database user
 d. Database owner
9 To retrieve data from DBMS is referred to as the

a. DML
b. DDL
c. SQL
d. Database language

10 Updating a database means
a. Revising the file structure
b. Modifying or adding a record
c. Reorganizing the database
d. Modifying the database

11 Identify not a valid relational database
a. IMS
b. ORACLE
c. Sybase
d. UNIFY

12 Data about data is called
a. Directory
b. Record
c. Metadata
d. Data Bank

13 Data dictionary stores the details of
a. The data types of all fields of all files
b. The names of all fields in all files
c. Both of the above
d. None of above

14 Data is a collection of
a. raw facts and Fig.s
b. The Electronic representation of facts
c. Information
d. None

15 The founder of the relational database
a. EF Codd
b. kahate
c. James Gossling
d. Dennies Rithchie

16 DBMS are not intended to
a. Eliminate data redundancy
b. Manage files access
c. Maintain data integrity
d. Separate files

17 Indicate an early development of relational model developed by E.F. Codd of IBM?
a. R:base
b. DB2
c. DBase-II
d. IDMS

18 Indicate noncomponent of a database
   a. Indexes
   b. Metadata
   c. Reports
   d. User data

Answers to MCQs:

1	2	3	4	5	6	7	8	9	10	11	12	13	14	15	16	17	18
A	C	A	B	D	C	A	A	C	B	D	C	A	A	A	D	B	C

Short and Long Answer Type Questions

1. List major steps in creating a database for an enterprise.
2. Illustrate major database components with the schema diagram for your college would maintain.
3. Imagine creating a video portal that is similar to YouTube. Think of the data in a system for processing files. Describe how each of these elements relates to the storage of actual video data as well as to the information that describes the video, such as the title, the user who uploaded it, tags, and the users who watched it.
4. Differentiate a traditional file processing system and a DBMS.
5. Describe the five major functionalities of a database administrator (DBA)?
6. Summarize the database architectures viz. two-tier and three-tier. Suggest a suited architecture for Web applications.
7. Identify three possible entities that could be utilized to store data in a social networking system like Facebook.
8. Outline the different types of database end users and their main activities for each

Numerical Problems

1. Refer to Fig. 1.2. If the department name changed to 'CSSE' from 'CS' and the corresponding course_number also needs to change. Identify the same columns in the database that need to be updated according to changes.

2. According to the above change, illustrate the schema diagram of restructured columns in the COURSE, SECTION, and PREREQUISITE relations so that only one column will need to be updated.

PRACTICAL

Analysis of Requirements

S Chand Publishing's proprietor offers a statement of his desires about: "My consumers to be able to explore my collection of books and place orders through Internet sources. I now only accept phone orders. Most of my callers are business clients who tells about the ***ISBN number and the quantity of books****. I then put together a delivery it includes the books ordered. I want to ship the customer's complete order, so if enough copies are not available on hand, and gets more number of orders then it leads to delay the shipment until the fresh copies come. I list all of my books in my catalogue. The catalogue includes the book details as title of the book, ISBN number, author name, purchase and sales price, and publication year. The majority of the clients are repeated customers, and have available records containing names, addresses, and credit_card information. Prior to using my website, brand-new clients must call me and create an account.*

Customers should first identify themselves on my new website using their specific customer identification number. Then, they ought to have access to my catalogue and be able to make purchases online.

The requirements phase was accomplished so rapidly that DBGig consultants takes weeks of discussions to get this done to analyze this information.

KNOW MORE

Edgar F. Codd, the creator of relational databases defined 13 properties of databases system that should possess in the year 1970 and developed further in a 1974 conference paper.

Dr Edgar F. Codd Rules [Relational Model of database systems with twelve rules]	Rule 1: Information Rule
	Rule 2: Guaranteed Access Rule
	Rule 3: Systematic Treatment of NULL Values
	Rule 4: Active Online Catalog
	Rule 5: Comprehensive Data Sub-Language Rule
	Rule 6: View Updating Rule
	Rule 7: High-Level Insert, Update, and Delete Rule
	Rule 8: Physical Data Independence
	Rule 9: Logical Data Independence
	Rule 10: Integrity Independence
	Rule 11: Distribution Independence
	Rule 12: Non-Subversion Rule

https://www.red-gate.com/simple-talk/databases/theory-and-design/codds-twelve-rules/

Commercial DB systems:

- IBM DB2 - www.ibm.com/software/data/db2
- Oracle - www.oracle.com
- Microsoft SQL Server - www.microsoft.com/sql
- Sybase - www.sybase.com
- IBM Informix - www.ibm.com/software/data/informix

Free/public domain database systems:

- MySQL - www.mysql.com
- PostgreSQL - www.postgresql.org

REFERENCES AND SUGGESTED READINGS

- Henry F Korth, Abraham Silberschatz, "Database system concepts", sixth ed., McGraw-Hill International editions, Computer Science Series
- Elmasri, Navathe, "Fundamentals of Database Systems", Elmasri, Navathe, Third ed, Addison Wesley
- Raghurama Krishnan, Johannes Gehrke, Database Management Systems, 3rd Edition, Tata McGraw Hill.
- C. J. Date, "An introduction to Database Systems", Sixth ed., Narosa Publications
- Database management systems- NPTEL: https://nptel.ac.in/courses/106105175

Dynamic QR Code for Further Reading

Further Reading about – DBMS: Database Design Process

Topics discussed:

1. Overview of the database design process
   a. Requirements Collection & Analysis.
   b. Functional Requirements.
   c. Conceptual Design.
   d. Logical Design/Data Model Mapping.
   e. Physical Design.
2. Weak Entity Types.
3. Symbols used in ER Diagram.
4. Sample Database Application (COMPANY).
5. Initial Conceptual Design of COMPANY Database.

https://www.youtube.com/watch?v=7m6gXeMDaHc

2 DATA MODELING

UNIT SPECIFICS

Through this unit we have discussed the following aspects:

- *Conceptual Modeling*
- *Example Database Application*
- *ER Model Concepts*
- *Data Modeling using the Entity-Relationship Model*
- *The Enhanced Entity-Relationship (EER) model*

The practical applications of the topics are discussed for generating further curiosity and creativity as well as to improve problem-solving capacity.

Besides giving a large number of multiple choice questions as well as questions of short and long answer types marked in two categories following lower and higher order of Bloom's taxonomy, assignments through several numerical problems, a list of references, and suggested readings are given in the unit so that one can go through them for practice. It is important to note that for getting more information on various topics of interest some QR codes have been provided in different sections which can be scanned for relevant supportive knowledge.

After the related practical, based on the content, there is a "Know More" section. This section has been carefully designed so that the supplementary information provided in this part becomes beneficial for the users of the book. This section mainly highlights the initial activity, examples of some interesting facts, analogy, history of the development of the subject focusing on the salient observations and finding, timelines starting from the development of the concerned topics up to the recent time, applications of the subject matter for our day-to-day real life or/and industrial applications on a variety of aspects, case study related to environmental, sustainability, social and ethical issues whichever applicable, and finally inquisitiveness and curiosity topics of the unit.

RATIONALE

This Data Modeling unit in Database systems helps students to get a primary idea about the real-time database applications, entity-relationship(ER) model, and extended entity-relationship model. It explains the need for data modeling, concepts, ER model of a sample application, relationships, and extended ER modelof the database system. All theseaspects are crucial for designing a database system implementation. It then explains clearly elements of ER model, a real time database model. All these are discussed at length to model the database systems. Some related case studies are pointed out with an extension to the data model, which can help further in getting a clear idea of the concern topics on database systems.

Databases are an important branch of computer science that essentially deals with information and data and their effect on information retrieval. Database system implementation needs as a prerequisite step data modeling and it is termed relational database management. This permits one to analyze the operations of many day-to-day transactions around us. Its practical applications are related to the model, construction, and operation of different types of database systems and tools.

PRE-REQUISITES

Mathematics: Calculus, Algebra (Class XII)
Computer Science: problem-solving with programming (Class XII)

UNIT OUTCOMES

The List of outcomes of this unit is as follows:

U2-O1: Summarize the elements of E-R diagrams to visualize the system at conceptual level.

U2-O2: Make use of Entity Relationship (ER) diagrams to design a database system.

U2-O3: Illustrate conceptual design using an ER diagram to represent a real-time database application.

U2-O4: Outline the enhanced entity-relationship (EER) diagramfeatures to implement the object-oriented features

U2-O5: Develop a database model with the help of ER/EER diagrams of real-time system

Unit-2 Outcomes	EXPECTED MAPPING WITH COURSE OUTCOMES (1-WeakCorrelation;2-Mediumcorrelation;3-StrongCorrelation)					
	CO-1	CO-2	CO-3	CO-4	CO-5	CO-6
U2-O1	3	1	3	-	-	-
U2-O2	1	1	1	-	-	-
U2-O3	2	2	3	-	-	-
U2-O4	3	3	3	-	-	-

U2-O5	3	3	3	-	-	-

2.1. CONCEPTUAL MODELING

In designing a database system, conceptual modeling plays a crucial role. After requirement analysis, the design of the database system is implemented in three levels conceptual, logical, and physical. The major phases in the database design process are illustrated in Fig.2.1.

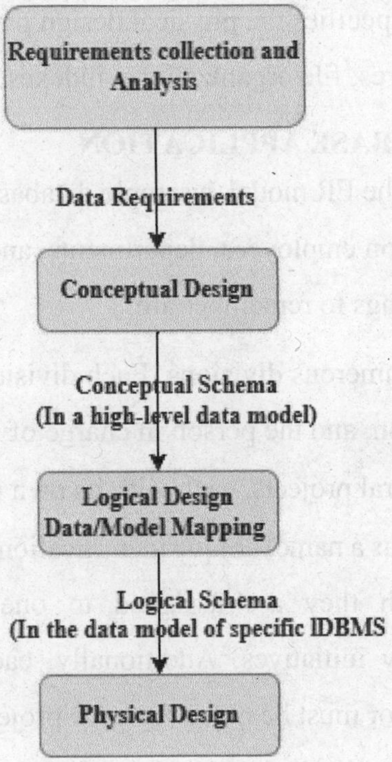

Fig. 2.1. Illustration of various phases in database design

Step 1: Requirement collection and analysis – database designers interview the prospective users and document the data requirements.

Step 2: Conceptual schema –a concise description of the data requirements of the users and details of entity types, relationships, and major constraints. The high-level user actions and queries observed during functional analysis can be specified either during or after the conceptual schema design via the fundamental data model operations.

Step 3: Logical Design/Data modeling mapping - a commercial database management system is used for an implementation data model such as a relational object-relational database model. Hence, a High-level conceptual model is transformed into an implementation model. Also called logical design or data model mapping.

Step 4: Physical design – It specifies the physical design parameters for the database files, internal storage structures, file organizations, indexes, and access paths.

2.2. AN EXAMPLE DATABASE APPLICATION

To demonstrate the ideas of the ER model, a sample database named the Industry database was used. Information on employees, departments, and projects can be found in this database. Important things to remember are:

- The Industry has numerous divisions. Each division is identified specifically by name, office location, and the person in charge of managing it.
- A division has several projects, each with its own name, number, and budget.
- Employee (EMP) has a name, unique identification number, residence, wage, and birthdate. Although they are assigned to one division, employees might participate in many initiatives. Additionally, each employee's start date and immediate supervisor must be noted for each project.
- Need to maintain each employee's dependents history with dependent_name, birthday, and relationship to the employee.

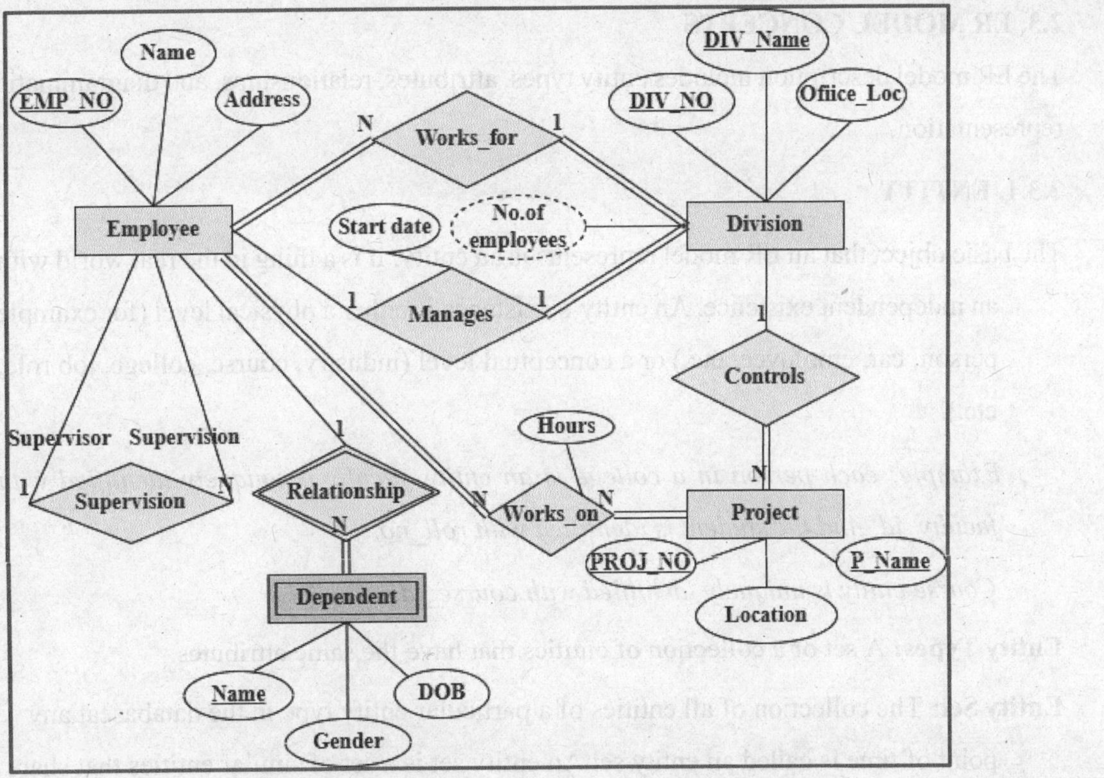

Fig. 2.2. ER Diagram of Sample Industry Data Model

The ER diagram of the sample industry data model is illustrated in Fig. 2.1. This illustration will be discussed as ER concepts in detail in further sections.

The major noting's of the diagram are listed as:

Major Entities: Employee, Division, Project, Dependent

Relationships: Work_for, Manages, Controls, Work_on, Supervision, Relationship

Entity – Attributes:

Entity	Attribute 1	Attribute 2	Attribute 3
Employee	Emp_No	Name	Address
Division	DIV_No	DIV_Name	Office_Loc
Project	Proj_No	P_Name	Location
Dependent	Name	Gender	DOB

2.3. ER MODEL CONCEPTS

The ER model description includes entity types, attributes, relationships, and diagrammatic representation.

2.3.1. ENTITY

The basic object that an ER model represents is an entity. It is a thing in the real world with an independent existence. An entity's existence is either a physical level (for example person, car, employee, etc.) or a conceptual level (industry, course, college, job role, etc.).

Example: each person in a college is an entity. faculty is uniquely identified with faculty_id. And the student is identified with roll_no.

Course entity is uniquely identified with course_id.

Entity Types: A set or a collection of entities that have the same attributes.

Entity Set: The collection of all entities of a particular entity type in the databaseat any point of time is called an entity set.An entity set is a set of similar entities that share the same properties, or attributes.

Example: Entity set faculty, is the set of all people, who are faculty at a given college.

The entity set student represents the set of all students in the university.

Weak Entity:

A weak entity can be identified uniquely only by considering the primary key of another (owner) entity. It does not have a single key attribute and it participate in a one-to-many relationship set (one owner, many weak entities). Weak entity set must have total participation in this identifying relationship set.

Example: In a college database, a subject is a strong entity and a course_offering can be modeled as a weak entity. The discriminator of course_offering would be semester (including year) and section_number (if there is more than one section)

If we model course_offering as a strong entity we would model course_number as an attribute.

2.3.2. ATTRIBUTE

Each entity has a set of attributes that describe the properties of objects. For example, an employee entity can describe with name, ID, age, department, location, contact no, address, salary, and designation. The attribute values of the entity become a major part of the database.

Each attribute has a set of allowable values called a domain, or valueset.

Example: Attribute Faculty may be described by the set *{(ID,* 101), (*name,* singh), (*deptname,* sales), (*salary,* 45000)*}*

Fig. 2.3 illustrates the two entities (employee EMP1; Industry IND1). Employee entity has a set of attributes EMP1(ID, NAME, ADDRESS, SALARY, DIVISION, CONTACT, AGE) with values (101, Singh, 201, lalbar, highroad), and industry IND1(Name, Head Quarters, CEO NAME) with Values(Reliance Industries, Mumbai, Ambani).

EMP1	ID=101
	NAME=Singh
	ADDRESS=201,lalbar,highroad
	SALARY=45000
	DIVISION=Sales
	CONTACT=9884453889
	AGE=43

IND1	Name=Reliance
	Head quaters=Mumbai
	CEO NAME=Ambani

Fig. 2.3. Two entities and their attributes with values

Types of Attributes:

The attributes of an entity are categorized based on values stored on it. They are

1. Simple – single unique valued attribute

2. Composite – more than one component

3. Single valued – single value attribute

4. Multi-Valued – more than one valued attribute

5. Stored – is used to derive a value to the derived attribute.

6. Derived – derived from existing attribute

7. NULL Value - The null value indicates not applicable, missing, or not known

Fig. 2.4 illustrates different types of attributes along with appropriate examples.

Type	Description
Simple	•Attributes that are not divisible further •Ex. Employee ID attribute always holds single value
Composite	•Composite attributes can be divided into smaller subparts, which represent more basic attributes with independent meanings. •Ex: Address attribute can be devided into **Street_address, City, State, and Zip**
Single valued	•Attribute having a single value for a particular entity •Ex: Attribute Age have a single vlaue for a employee
Multi-valued	•An attribute can have a set of values for the same entity •Ex: College degrees have multi values •May have lower and upper bounds to constrain the number of values allowed for each individual entity
Stored	•The stored attribute value is used to define a derived attribute. •Ex: Birth_Date of a person
Derived	•two (or more) attribute values are interrelated •Ex: the Age and Birth_date attributes of a person. •For a particular person entity, the value of Age can be determined from the current (today's) date and the value of that person's Birth_date •Hence, The Age attribute is called a derived attribute and is said to be derivable from the Birth_date attribute
NULL Values	•An attribute may not have an appropriate value due to either not applicable or not availble. •Ex. Flat No attribute is NULL for cases of indipendent houses.
Complex	•The complex attribute is a combination of composite and multivalued. The composite attribute values between parentheses () by separating the components with commas, and multivalued attributes between braces { }.

Fig. 2.4. List of various types of attributes with appropriate examples

Examples of different attributes

Faculty ID is a single valued attribute.

Faculty_contact is a multi-valued attribute, it holds zero, one, or more number of phone numbers. Is represented in {value1, value2, value3}

Faculty_mentors is a derived attribute, is derived from the count of students associated with mentor.

Faculty Name is a Composite attribute (Firstname, Middlename and Lastname) and composite hierarchy attribute as address (street, city, state, pin_code) and street (St_name, St_name, apartment_no) is represented in Fig. 2.5.

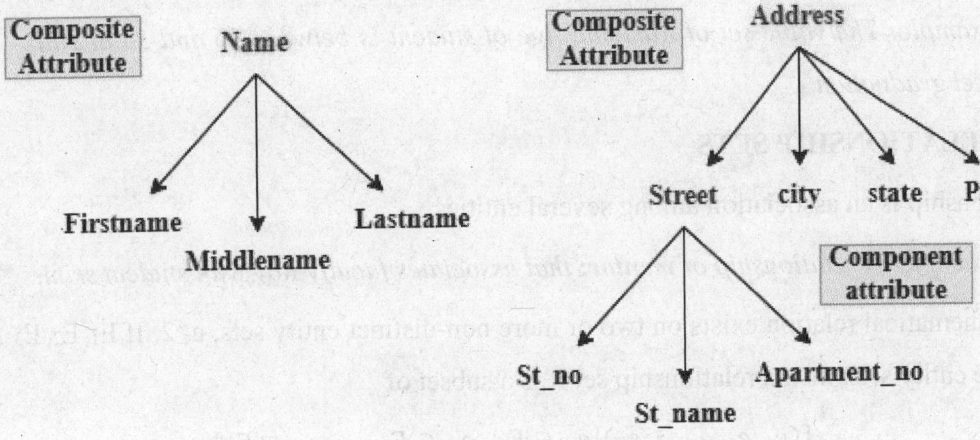

Fig. 2.5. Example of composite attribute

2.3.3. KEYS

A constraint on the entities of an entity type is the key or uniqueness constraint on attributes. An entity has one or more attributes whose values are distinct in the entity set. Such an attribute is called a key attribute, and its values can be used to identify each entity uniquely.

Value Sets (or Domains): Value Sets (Domains) of attributes of an entity type are associated with a value set (or domain of values), which specifies the set of values that may be assigned to that attribute for each individual entity.

The mathematical representation of an entity set E of an attribute A whose value set is V can be defined as a function from E to the power set P(V) of V:

$$A : E \rightarrow P(V)$$

The value set provides all possible values of an attribute.

For single-valued or multi-valued and NULL valued attribute is represented as power set P(V).

single-valued attribute: A(e) is a single value set of the respective entity. Multy-valued attribute: A(e) is a power set of entity e.

Example: The value set of Attribute Age of student is between 16 and 35 at entry-level graduation

2.3.4. RELATIONSHIP SETS

A relationship is an association among several entities.

Example: A relationship of ***mentor:*** *that associates faculty Roy with student srini.*

The mathematical relation exists on two or more non-distinct entity sets, n≥2. If E_1, E_2, E_3 are entity sets, then a relationship set R is a subset of

$$\{(e_1, e_2, e_3 \ldots . e_n) | e_1 \in E_1,\ e_2 \in E_2 \ldots . . e_n \in E_n\}$$

Where $(e_1, e_2, e_3 \ldots . e_n)$ is a relationship. The association between entity sets E1, E2, . . ., En participate in the relationship set R.

Example: A relationship of ***enrolled****: that depicts the relationship between a student and his enrolled subject section. Here the two entities student and subject section are in binary relationship set i.e advisor.*

Constraints: The E-R schema defines the set of constraints to which the database contents must follow. This is represented in mapping cardinalities and constraints.

2.3.5. MAPPING CARDINALITIES

Mapping cardinalities will direct the total number of entities that a relationship set can be used to link one entity to another. Although they can help with the description of relationship sets that include more than two entity sets, mapping cardinalities are most helpful when expressing binary relationship sets. The mapping cardinality of binary relationship set R between entity sets A and B are given in Fig. 2.6.

One-to-one: An entity in A is associated with at most one entity in B, and an entity in B is associated with at most one entity in A.

One-to-many: An entity in A is associated with any number (zero or more) of entities in B. An entity in B can be associated with at most one entity in A.

Many-to-one. An entity in A is associated with at most one entity in B. An entity in B can be associated with any number (zero or more) of entities in A.

Many-to-many. An entity in A is associated with any number (zero or more) of entities in B, and an entity in B is associated with any number (zero or more) of entities in A.

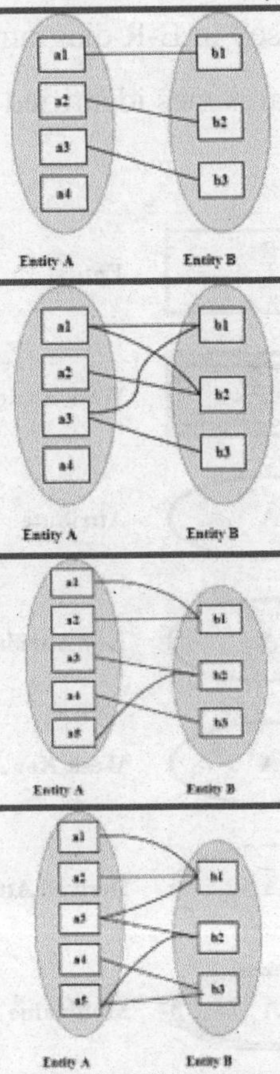

Fig. 2.6. Mapping Cardinalities

2.3.6. STANDARD NOTATIONS FOR ER DIAGRAMS

Fig. 2.7 summarizes the various components used in conceptual design using E-R diagrams. The Entity Relationships (E-R) diagram components are:

1. Rectangle - represents entities.
2. Diamond – symbolize a relationships among entities, and are connected to the Rectangles(entities) by lines with cardinality lables.
3. Ellipse - symbolize an attribute, and are linked to the entities or relationships.
4. Line – symbolize a link between an attribute to entity and entity to relationships.

The symbols used in E-R diagrams (rectangle, diamond and ellipse) are labelled with the conceptual names identified as an entity, relationship set, and attribute respectively.

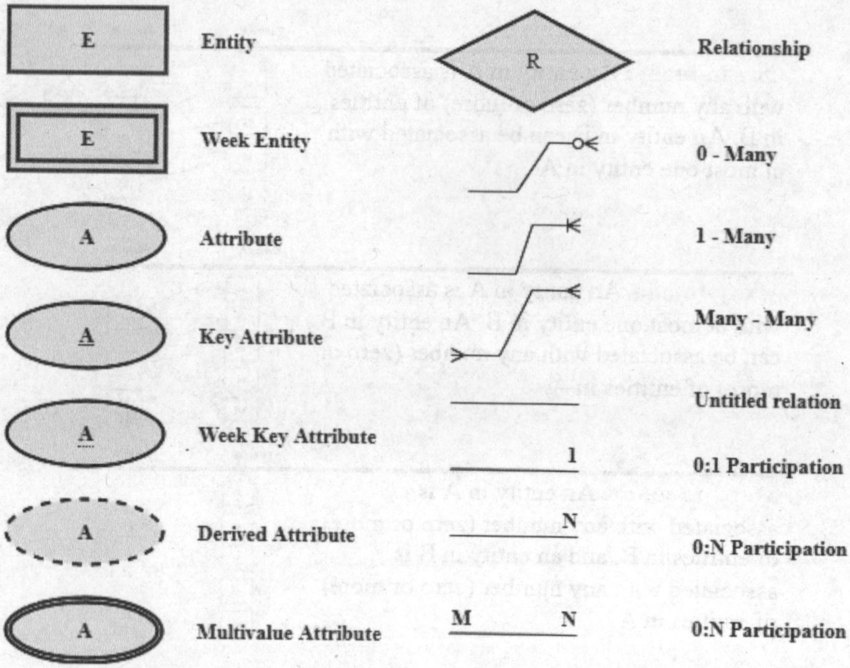

Fig. 2.7. Summary of notations for ER Diagrams (Symbol – Meaning)

2.3.7. CASE STUDY – LIBRARY MANAGEMENT SYSTEM

An example system would be a Library Management System having the following factors are taken into account while tracking readers in the database:

A single point authentication system that consists of a login ID and password, the system maintains the track of the staff logs.

The library staff updates the book collection with information on each title's ISBN, price in Indian rupees, category types (general, innovations, story), edition number, and unique author number.

A publisher has a publisher ID number, the booktitle, and the year it was published.

Member register by providing a member ID, MailId, member name (firstname and lastname), contact number (multiple numbers are permitted), and contact address. The library staff monitors the readers.

Books that have the issue and return date stamped can be considered as reserved by readers. It can have a due date as well if it is not returned within the allotted time frame.

The conceptual design of the library management system (LMS) in Entity- Relationship model with E-R diagram is presented in the following steps:

Step 1: Recognize the strong entity set and week entity set

Step 2: Identify the related attributes to each entity

Step 3: Identify the relationship sets

Step 4: Detect the mapping cardinalities and participation of entities

Step 1: Strong and Week entity sets Entity - 1: Book Entity - 2: Member Entity - 3: Publisher Entity - 4: Authentication Entity - 5: Staff	**Step 2: Related attributes of each identified entity** **Book**: Book_Id, auther_no, ISBN_no, Title of the book, edition_no, category_type, price. ISBN_no is the Key attribute. **Member**: Member_Id, Mail_Id, address, Contact_no, Mem_name. Mem_Name is a composite attribute of first_name and last_name. Contact_no is multi-valued attribute. member_Id is the Key attribute for the member entity. Publisher_details: Publisher_Id, YOP, name. Publisher_ID is the Key attribute. Authentication: Login_Id and PSW. Login_ID is a key attribute. Report: Member_Id, Registration_no, Book_Id, Issue/Return date. Reg_no is the key attribute of report. Lib_Staff: staff_id and Name. staff_id is a key attribute. Reserve/Return set : Resdate, Duedate, and Retdate.
Step 3: Relationship sets between entities R -1: Reserve: A reader can reserve books. R-2: publish: A Publisher can publish books. R - 3: track: staff track the readers. R – 4: maintain: multiple reports and books R – 5: provides: multiple logins for staff.	**Step 4: Constraints and participation** A member can reserve - N books but one book can be reserved by one member. Hence the mapping cardinality is1:N. A publisher will publish any number of books but a book is published by only one publisher. Hence the mapping cardinality is 1:N. The staff track of readers. Here the mapping cardinality is M:N. Staff maintains multiple reports and books. The mapping cardinality is1:N. Authentication - responsible for login to multiple staff. The mapping cardinality is1:N.

The detailed conceptual design of the library management system in E-R diagram is illustrated in Fig. 2.8.

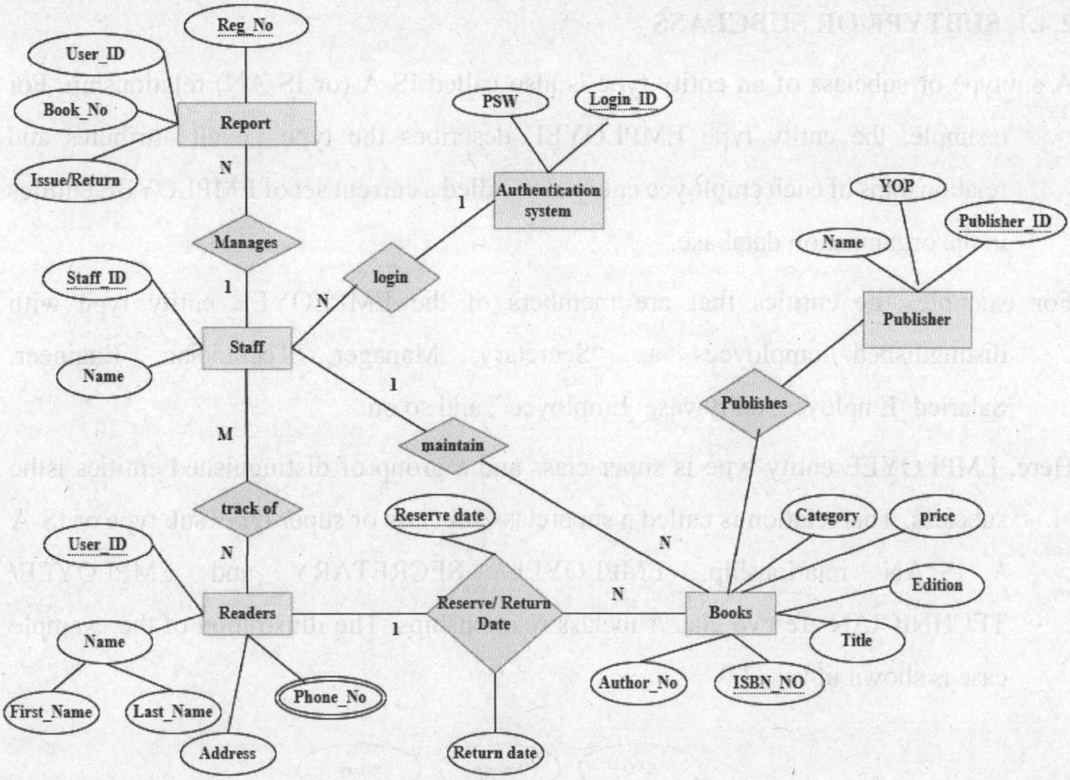

Fig. 2.8. Illustration of Conceptual design of the library management system using E-R diagram

2.4. ENHANCED ENTITY RELATIONSHIP (EER) MODEL CONCEPTS

The Enhanced E-R model includes all E-R model concepts and the concepts of subclass and super class and the related concepts of specialization and generalization. Another concept included in the EER model is that of a category or union type, which is used to represent a collection of objects (entities) that is the union of objects of different entity types. Associated with these concepts is the important mechanism of attribute and relationship inheritance.

2.4.1. SUBTYPE OR SUBCLASS

A subtype or subclass of an entity type is also called IS-A (or IS-AN) relationship. For example, the entity type EMPLOYEE describes the type i.e all attributes and relationships of each employee entity also called a current set of EMPLOYEE entities in the organization database.

For example, the entities that are members of the EMPLOYEE entity type with distinguished employees as "Secretary, Manager, Technician, Engineer, Salaried_Employee, dailywase_Employee", and so on.

Here, EMPLOYEE entity type is super class and a group of distinguished entities isthe subclass. This relation is called a superclass/subclass or super type/ sub type or IS-A / IS_AN relationship. EMPLOYEE/ SECRETARY and EMPLOYEE/ TECHNICIAN are two class/subclass relationships. The illustration of the example case is shown in Fig. 2.9.

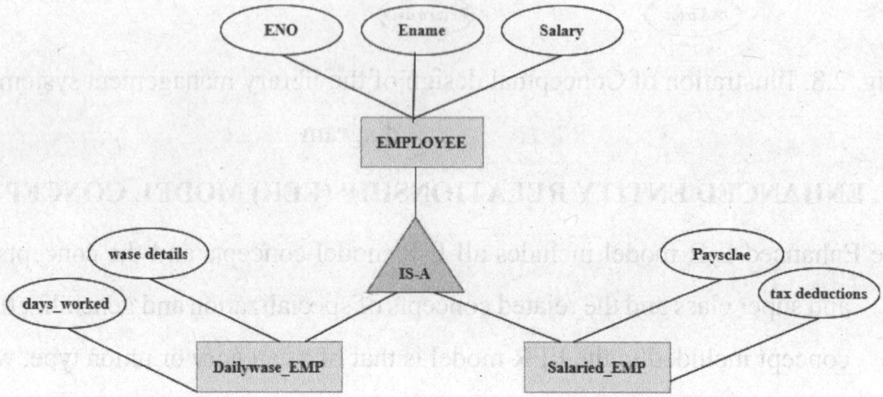

Fig. 2.9. A Concept of IS_A relationship in Enhanced E-R Model

2.4.2. SPECIALIZATION, GENERALIZATION AND LATTICES

The process of designating subgroupings within an entity set is called specialization. The specialization of employee allows distinguishing among employees based on roles as {technician, manager, secretary, engineer}, a employee entity is any of these types. The commonality among all employees is referred as generalization.

In Fig. 2.9, the employee entity having attributes such as eno, name, and salary are common among all entities. Hence this entity is a generalization. Whereas the entities daily wase, salaries are specialized entities having a unique set of attributes along with employee entity attributes.

UNIT SUMMARY

The design of the database system is implemented in three levels:

- Conceptual
- Logical, and
- Physical.

The major phases in the database design process are:

- Requirement collection and analysis
- Conceptual schema
- Logical Design/Data modeling mapping
- Physical design

The ER model description includes terms like:

- Entity set
  - Week entity and
  - Strong entity
- Attributes
  - Simple attribute
  - Composite attribute
  - Single valued attribute
  - Multi-Valued attribute
  - Stored attribute
  - Derived attribute
  - NULL Value
- Relationships
  - One to one
  - One to many
  - Many to one
  - Many to many

Diagrammatic representation – E-R Diagrams with standard components.

- Enhanced E-R Diagrams
  - IS-A relationship
  - Generalisation
  - Specialization

Conceptual Data Modeling using E-R Model

Consider the Insurance Plan Management System, a well-known and widespread issue in the modern world. For this issue, the Software Requirements Specifications (SRS) are as follows:

1. *The Insurance Provider includes numerous branches, each of which has a branchid, branch name, and/or address, location, contact information, fax, etc.*
2. *There are several staff members employed in each branch. For illustration, there is a Manager, field agents, staff members who work in development, secretarial assistants, etc. It keeps track of staff members' names, addresses, positions, salaries, and dates of employment or birth.*
3. *In addition to full-time employees, there are part-time workers known as insurance agents who are commission-based employees.*
4. *The insurance provider is required to keep policyholder information on file. the policyholder address, tenure, maturity amount, policy number, and name*

With the knowledge of E-R diagrams studied so far, Identify the entity types, attributes related to entity and relationships.

EXERCISES

Multiple Choice Questions

1 ……………..indicates the max. no. of entities existed in a relationship?
A. Greater Entity Count
B. Maximum cardinality
C. Entity Relationship Diagram
D. Minimum cardinality

2 ………….is an association among entities in an E-R model.
A. Record
B. Relationship
C. Field
D. Tuple

3 ……….. entity is a part of a one-to-many relationship.
A. Instance
B. Child
C. Parent
D. Subtype

4 ……..entity is associated with the generalization of EER.
A. Archetype
B. Supertype
C. Subtype
D. Instance

5 A specialization relation of EERD may also known as………………..
A. Super-Sub
B. Sub-Super
C. Lower relation
D. Higher relation

6 ………….. indicates the min. no. of entities involved in a relationship.
A. Entity Relationship Diagram
B. Maximum_cardinality
C. Minimum_cardinality
D. Greater Entity Count

7 Mapping cardinality of relations in E-R diagram are describing about
A. composite
B. unary
C. simple
D. binary

8 In ERD illustrations, specialization is represented with
A. solid arrow
B. double arrow

C. hallow arrow

D. dashed arrow

9 ....relationship is existed between the week entity and the identified entity set.

A. dependency

B. existence

C. Identifying

D. dependency

10 .... is used to represent a strong entity in E-R diagram

A. rectangle

B. rhombus

C. oval

D. double-bordered rectangle

11 ....is used to represent a multivalued attribute in E-R diagram

A. oval

B. double lined rhombus

C. double lined oval

D. double-bordered rectangle

12 An employee works in the sales department. In this, works relationship exists with a cardinality of

A. 1-1

B. 1-N

C. N-1

D. M-N

13 The mentor mentors the students in a college. In this, mentors relationship exists with a cardinality of

A. 1-1

B. 1-N

C. N-1

D. M-N

14 A customer has a loan account. In this, has a relationship exists with

A. 1-1

B. 1-N

C. N-1

D. M-N

15 Contact information is ....type of attribute

A. single
B. multi
C. NULL
D. derived

16 BMI value is ....type of attribute
A. single
B. multi
C. NULL
D. derived

17 Speed is ....type of attribute
A. single
B. multi
C. NULL
D. derived

18 In a student entity set, the undergraduate students are represented with...... relationship
A. IS-AN
B. generalization
C. entity set
D. specialization

Answers to MCQs:

1	2	3	4	5	6	7	8	9	10	11	12	13	14	15	16	17	18
B	B	A	B	A	C	A	B	C	D	C	A	B	B	B	D	D	D

Short and Long Answer Type Questions

1. Distinguish strong-entity with weak-entity?
2. Illustrate the major E-R components used to represent the conceptual view of the database system.
3. Imagine creating a video portal that is similar to YouTube. Think of the data in a system for processing files. Describe how each of these elements relates to the storage of actual video data as well as to the information that describes the video, such as the title, the user who uploaded it, tags, and the users who watched it.
4. Construct an ER-Diagram for a hospital management system with a set of patients and medical doctors. A patient log contains a history of tests conducted and consultations made.

5. Construct an E-R diagram for maintaining a track of the sports team based on interest. Then a system should store the matches played, the scores in each match, the players in each match and individual player statistics for each match. Summary statistics should be modeled as derived attributes.
6. List the different types of attributes with significant examples.
7. Identify three possible entities and related attributes that could be utilized to maintain the attributes of a social networking system like LinkedIn.
8. Outline the different types of data modeling techniques and their phases to develop a database system.
9. Summarize the Enhanced Entity Relationship model concepts with cars example.

Numerical Problems

1.It has been determined by Amazon.com to rearrange its database. Books, sales, and user data are all stored. Amazon collects as much data as it can on user behaviour so that it can analyse it and make site improvements. Here are a few prerequisites:

(a) Each user is assigned a special ID, name, password, and email address. Amazon emails consumers on a regular basis, thus it's crucial to know if the user is okay with being spammed and if their email address has been returning messages.

(b) Amazon keeps track of a user's most recent visit date so that it can show the user a list of products that have been added to the site since his previous visit.

(c) Books are identified by their ISDN number, title, author, publisher, and 2. According to the above change, illustrate the schema diagram of restructured columns in the COURSE, SECTION, and PREREQUISITE relationsso that only one column will need to be updated.

To model the above-mentioned data, create an E-R diagram. Recall to include constraints, important attributes, etc. Mention all presumptions, all required logical assumptions.

PRACTICAL

1. A bank wants to automate each transaction. It provides the subsequent account types: Fixed Deposit(FD), Recurring Deposit(RD), and Savings Bank (SB)

The Bank also wants to monitor the loans granted to its clients. Determine the entities, their properties, and any relationships among them.

Draw the ER diagram using any open source tool and make sure to provide all explicit assumptions. Consider the following presumptions:

a. A customer is limited to having a single type of account. Joint accounts are not permitted

b. Only when a consumer has at least one of the account kinds is a loan available.

2. To represent the requirements of a small computer business corporation, create an entity-relationship diagram:

a. The company's workers assemble several computer models. Each employee's employee number, name, address, phone number, job title, and salary are all kept on file.

b. The model, specifications, name, and quantity of each machine are also kept on file.

c. Each machine is made up of various components. The parts that are on hand must be listed in an inventory. A record of each part's name, cost, and available quantity is kept.

d. These components are purchased from a number of providers. The supplier's name, address, and phone number must be kept on file.

Computers that have been assembled are sold.

KNOW MORE

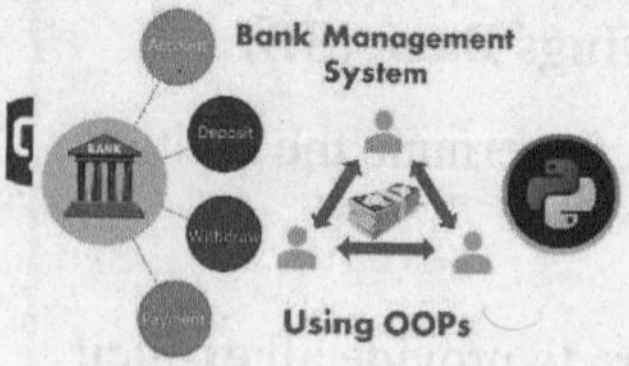

Drawing Entity Relationship (E-R) diagram of Banking Management system

https://www.youtube.com/watch?v=RVyCJXn--jY&ab_channel=TechnonTechTV

Free/public domain online Entity Relationship model Tools:

- Visual paradigm - https://online.visual-paradigm.com/diagrams/features/erd-tool/
- Smart draw - https://www.smartdraw.com/entity-relationship-diagram/er-diagram-tool.htm
- Lucid chart - https://www.lucidchart.com/pages/examples/er-diagram-tool
- Draw.io - https://drawio-app.com/entity-relationship-diagrams-with-draw-io/

REFERENCES AND SUGGESTED READINGS

- Henry F Korth, Abraham Silberschatz, “Database system concepts”, sixth ed., McGraw-Hill International editions, Computer Science Series
- Elmasri, Navathe,"Fundamentals of Database Systems", Elmasri, Navathe,Third ed, Addison Wesley
- Raghurama Krishnan, Johannes Gehrke, Database Management Systems, 3rd Edition, Tata McGraw Hill.
- C.J.Date, "An introduction to Database Systems", Sixth ed., NarosaPublications
- Database management systems- NPTEL: https://nptel.ac.in/courses/106105175

Dynamic QR Code for Further Reading

Further Reading about –Tool demonstration to build ER model is represented in draw.io

Topics discussed:

- Building entity sets and related attribute set
- Describing primary key and foreign key attributes of each entity
- Defining derived attributes based on requirement
- Identifying and modifying relationships existed among entity
- Altering cardinalities
- Defining weak entities

https://www.youtube.com/watch?v=lAtCySGDD48&ab_channel=Dr.DanielSoper

3 RELATIONAL MODEL AND FORMAL QUERY

UNIT SPECIFICS

Through this unit we have discussed the following aspects:

- *Relational Data Model Concepts*
- *Relational Database Constraints*
- *Mapping of ER/EER diagrams to Relational Model*
- *Formal query languages - Relational Algebra and Calculus*

The practical applications of the topics are discussed for generating further curiosity and creativity as well as to improve problem-solving capacity.

Besides giving a large number of multiple choice questions as well as questions of short and long answer types marked in two categories following lower and higher order of Bloom's taxonomy, assignments through several numerical problems, a list of references, and suggested readings are given in the unit so that one can go through them for practice. It is important to note that for getting more information on various topics of interest some QR codes have been provided in different sections which can be scanned for relevant supportive knowledge.

After the related practical, based on the content, there is a "Know More" section. This section has been carefully designed so that the supplementary information provided in this part becomes beneficial for the users of the book. This section mainly highlights the initial activity, examples of some interesting facts, analogy, history of the development of the subject focusing on the salient observations and finding, timelines starting from the development of the concerned topics up to the recent time, applications of the subject matter for our day-to-day real life or/and industrial applications on a variety of aspects, case study related to environmental, sustainability, social and ethical issues whichever applicable, and finally inquisitiveness and curiosity topics of the unit.

RATIONALE

This Relational modeling unit on Database systems helps students to get a basic idea of mapping of conceptual design to logical design on the real-time database applications and mathematical tools to perform query processing. It explains the logical design of the system using relational modelling and formal query languages like relational algebra and calculus are declarative query languages built on mathematical logic. All these basic mathematical functions are related tobuild query strings in commercial databases using SQL. All these are discussed at length to develop the database systems. Some related case studies are pointed out with an extension to the data model and schema development, which can help further in getting a clear idea of the concern topics on database systems.

Databases are an important branch of computer science that essentially deals with information and data and their effect on information retrieval. Structured query language (SQL) statements are started their journey by mathematical functions using calculus and algebra and then explaining it in terms of relational database management. This permits one to analyze the operations of many day-to-day transactions around us. Its practical applications are related to the relationalmodel construction and operation of different types of database systems and tools.

PRE-REQUISITES

Mathematics: Calculus, Algebra (Class XII)
Computer Science: problem-solving with programming (Class XII)

UNIT OUTCOMES

The List of outcomes of this unit is as follows:

U3-O1: Summarize the Relational modeling components to represent the system at a logical level.

U3-O2: Realize the need and importance of relational data model for implementation with commercial database systems.

U3-O3: Illustrate logical design using relational representations of a real-time database application

U3-O4: Interpret the database system with schemas in relational algebra and calculus

Unit-3 Outcomes	***EXPECTED MAPPING WITH COURSE OUTCOMES*** *(1-WeakCorrelation;2-Mediumcorrelation;3-StrongCorrelation)*					
	CO-1	***CO-2***	***CO-3***	***CO-4***	***CO-5***	***CO-6***
U3-O1	3	1	3	-	-	-
U3-O2	1	1	1	-	-	-
U3-O3	2	2	3	-	-	-

U3-O4	3	3	3	-	-	-

3.1. RELATIONAL DATA MODEL

The logical and view models are described with relational model. It provides the conceptualizing of low-level details of data storage. The higher-level data model discussed later in Chapter 2, entity-relationship(E-R)model is widely used for database design. The relational data model is a basic model for commercial data processing applications.

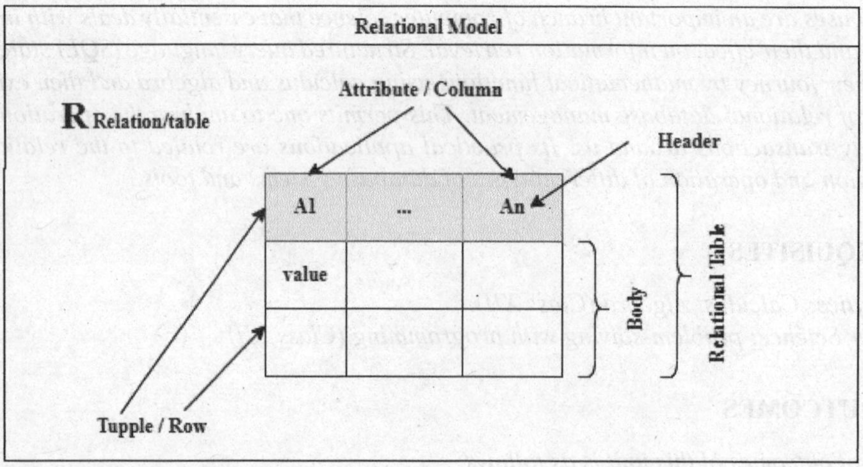

Fig. 3.1. Basic structure of a relational model

Fig. 3.1 illustrates the basic structure of a relational data model. The basic terminology includes relation (table), Attribute (column), and the values of each attribute are termed as tuples (row).

3.1.1. RELATIONAL MODEL CONCEPTS

Domain: A set of atomic values is termed a Domain. It is useful to interpret the value by a specific name in the domain. Each domain is specified with name, data type and design.

Examples of Domains:

AADHAAR Number – is a 12-digit number considered as a unique identity to all residents of India.

PIN Number – a six digit number refers to "Postal Index Number (PIN)", or PIN code to the Indian postal code system used by India.

INDIA_contact number – a set of 10-digit number valid in India.

Student_age – an integer value between 15 to 60 admission in higher education (preferably).

DEPT_name – The set of unique departmental codes is represented as CSE,ECE, EEE.

Relation: A relation R is described with a set of Attributes.

A Relation schema is indicated as R (A1, A2, ……An) and the degree of relation as a no. of attributes n of relation and is a set of m-tuples r = {t1, t2, ..., tm}. And a tuple t is t is a list of m values t =<v1, v2, ..., vm>.

Example: Student Relation is described as

STUDENT (Student_name, RollNo, Contact_No, Address, gender, age, GPA)

The definition is elaborated with specific datatypes

STUDENT (Student_name: String, RollNo: Integer, Contact_No: Integer, Address: String, gender: String, age: Integer, GPA: Real)

A relational database consists of set of tables(relations). Each table is constituted with set columns and rows. Each column is Attribute. And Each row is a tuple or a database record.

In relation student, first attribute is Student_name, the Second attribute is RollNo, etc

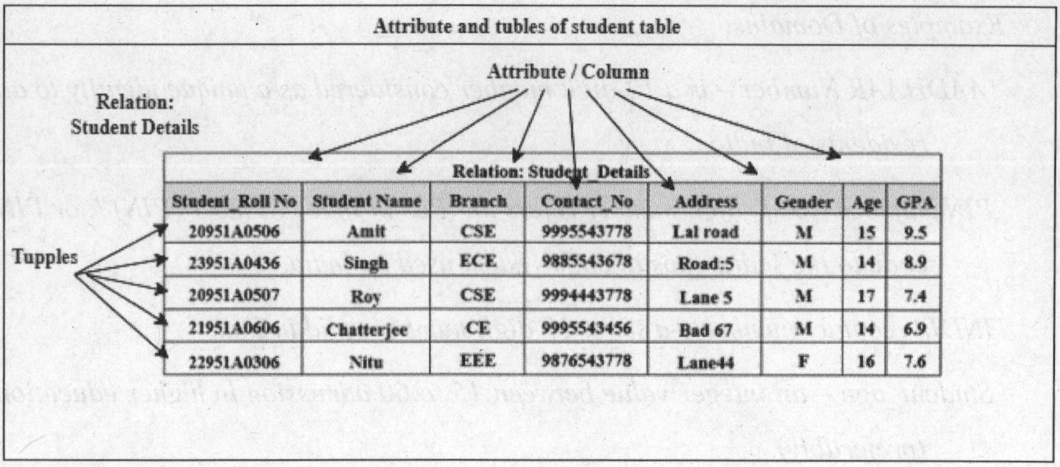

Student_Roll No	Student Name	Branch	Contact_No	Address	Gender	Age	GPA
20951A0506	Amit	CSE	9995543778	Lal road	M	15	9.5
23951A0436	Singh	ECE	9885543678	Road:5	M	14	8.9
20951A0507	Roy	CSE	9994443778	Lane 5	M	17	7.4
21951A0606	Chatterjee	CE	9995543456	Bad 67	M	14	6.9
22951A0306	Nitu	EEE	9876543778	Lane44	F	16	7.6

Fig. 3.2. Student relation with sample data of 5 tuples

Fig. 3.2 illustrates a sample table of student details. It exists 8 attributes(columns) and 5 tuples (rows) of unique student details.

Database Schema - is the logical design of the database

***Example**: Schema of the department:*

Department(Dept_name, location, budget)

Schema of the section:

Section(course_code, section_no, sem, year, room_no, location, time_slot)

Database Instance –Itis a snapshot of the data at a given instant in timein the database.

Sample instance of section table is shown in Fig. 3.3.

Section_No	Course Code	Semester	Year	Room_no	location	Time_slot
8	CS0321	Even	2018	1101	AB block	1
7	CS0101	Odd	2021	1108	AB block	3
5	CS0102	odd	2013	2109	BB block	5
1	HS101	odd	2022	2109	BB block	5
3	ES101	odd	2022	2109	BB block	5
2	BS101	Even	2022	2109	AB block	2
4	CS301	Even	2022	2109	AB block	4

Fig. 3.3 Database instance of section table

3.2. RELATIONAL DATABASE CONSTRAINTS

The restrictions or constraints on the database are derived from the rules of the specific organization. The constraints are categorized into three main categories.

1. Implicit constraints
2. Explicit constraints
3. Semantic constraints

Implicit Constraints – inherent in the data model. Also called model-based constraints.

Explicit Constraints – incorporated in the schema definition. Also called schema-based constraints.

Semantic Constraints–these are not expressed at the schema level and are enforced by the application-specific programs.

The schema-based constraints include domain, key constraints, null, and integrity constraints (entity and referential).

Fig. 3.4 lists the constraints in relational databases. These are implemented through Data Definition Language (DDL) and data types. The constraints on relational databases are implemented in four ways:

1. Domain level
2. Key level
3. Entity Integrity level
4. Referential integrity level

Super key- a set of one or more attributes whose values are guaranteed to identify tuples in the relation uniquely.

Candidate key - a minimal set of superkey of a relation,

Primary key - One of the candidate keys of a relation

Constraint	Description
Domain Constraint	• Standard numeric data types • Integers - short integer, integer, and long integer and real numbers - float and doubleprecision float • Characters, Booleans, fixed-length strings, and • Variable-length strings - date, time, timestamp, and money, or other special data types.
Key constraint	• Unique constrraints • Super Key - specifies uniqueness constraint • Candicdate Key - multiple keys • Primary Key - having not null
Entity Integrity constraint	• Primary key - should not hold null values.
Referencial Integrity Constraint	• Specified between two relations or tables • Rferential key of R1 is a Primary key of relation R2, then the referencial key of R1 will refer the relation R2.

Fig. 3.4. Kinds of Constraints on relational databases

3.3. ER/EER TO RELATIONAL MODEL MAPPING

Entity Relationship (E-R) model and Enhanced Entity Relationship (EER) model at conceptual design is mapped with the relational model at the logical level in three steps:

Step 1: Strong entities with simple and complex attributes

Step 2: Week entities

Step 3: Relationships

3.3.1. CASE STUDY: THE CONCEPTUAL DESIGN OF THE INDUSTRY DATABASE

Case study 1: The conceptual design of the Industry database in Entity-Relationship model with E-R diagram is presented in Fig. 3.5. Create a logical design by mapping with E-R diagram.

Mapping of ER/EER model to relational model is demonstrated on the ER diagram of Industry database.

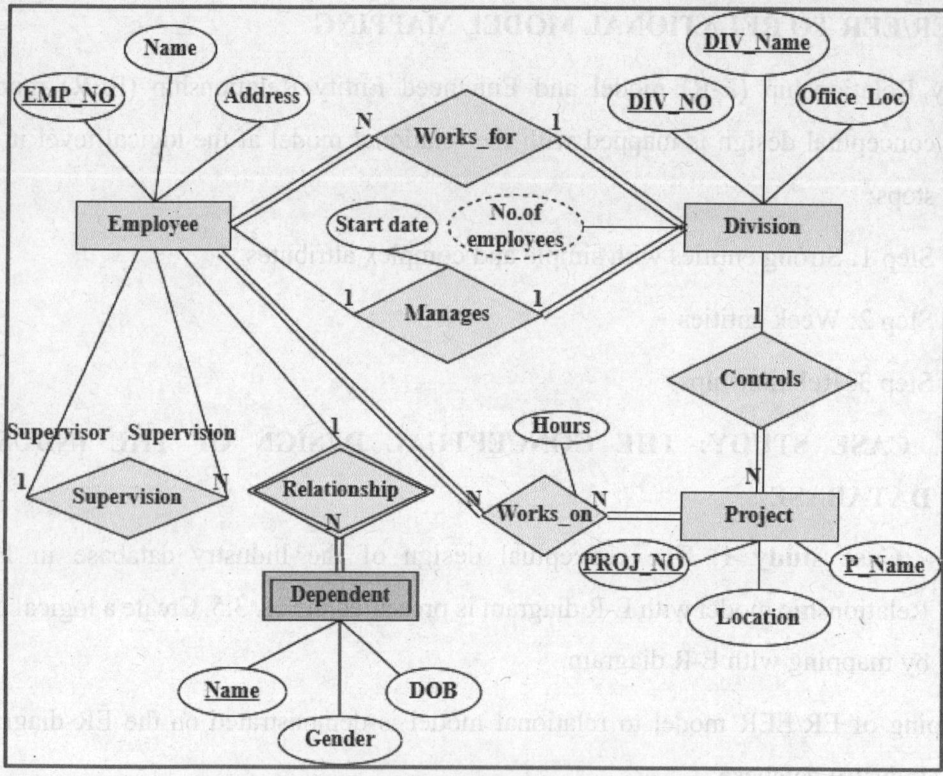

Fig. 3.5. ER diagram of Industry database.

Entities Sets with related attributes:

E1 – Employee (EMP_NO, Name, Address)

E2 – Dependent (Name, Gender, DOB)

E3 – Project (PROJ_NO, Location, P_Name

E4 – Division (DIV_NO, DIV_Name, Off_Loc)

Relationships sets

R1 – Supervision (Employee, Employee)

R2 – Relationship (Employee, Dependent)

R3 – Controls (Division, Project)

R4 – Manages (Employee, Division)

Employee

EMP_No	Name	Address

Dependent

Name	Gender	DOB

Division

DIV_NO	DIV_Name	Off_Loc

Project

Project_No	P_Name	Location

Fig. 3.6. Relational schemas identified from E-R diagram

Entity sets are represented as relational schema are shown in Fig. 3.6.

Schemas derived from relationship sets:

Supervision (Emp_Id, Emp_Id)

Relationship (Emp_Id, Name)

Controls (DIV_No, Project_No)

Manages (Emp_Id, DIV_No)

3.3.2. CASE STUDY: THE CONCEPTUAL DESIGN OF THE INDUSTRY DATABASE

Case study 2: The conceptual design of the library management system (LMS) in Entity- Relationship model with E-R diagram is presented in Fig. 3.7. Create a logical design by mapping with E-R diagram.

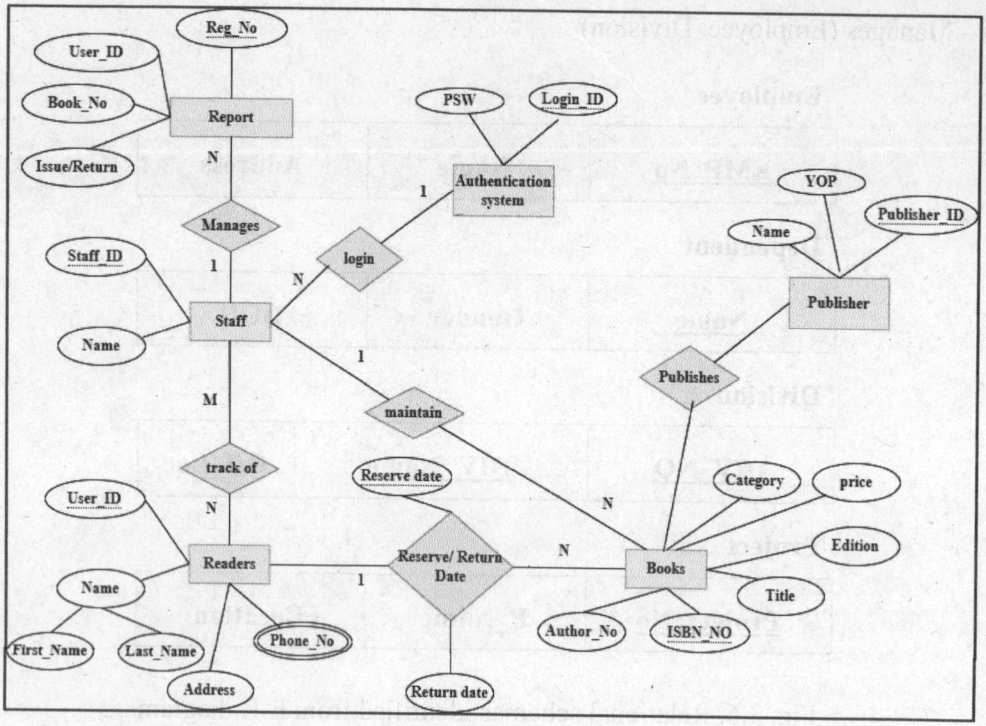

Fig. 3.7. E-R diagram of library management system (LMS)

Entities Sets with related attributes:

E - 1: Books (<u>Author_No</u>, <u>ISBN_No</u>, Title, Edition, Price, Category)

Complex attributes

E - 2: Readers (<u>User_ID</u>, Name, First_Name, Last, Name, Phone_No,Address)

E - 3: Publisher (Year, YOP, <u>Publisher_ID</u>)

E - 4: Authentication (<u>Login_Id</u>, PSW)

E - 5: Staff (<u>Staff_Id,</u> Name)

Relationships sets

R - 1: Reserve (User_Id, Reserve date, ISBN_NO)

R - 2: Publish (.Publisher_ID, ISBN_NO)

R - 3: track (Staff_Id, User_Id)

R - 4: maintain (Staff_ID, ISBN_NO)

R - 5: provides (Login_Id, Staff_Id).

3.4. RELATIONAL ALGEBRA

Relational algebra is a procedural query language. It defines a set of operations such as addition, subtraction, or multiplication. Usually, algebraic operations on numbers will take one or more numbers as input and return a number as output. The relational algebra will take one or more relations as input and return a relation as output.

The operations in algebra are:

Fundamental operations – project, select, difference, union, Cartesian_product, and rename

Other operations - set intersection, natural join, and assignment.

Comparison Operators

(a) < Less than

(b) > Greater than

(c) = Equal to

(d) Not equal to

(e) Lessthan or equal to

(f) Greaterthan or equal to

(g) use boolean operator "not" to negate a condition.

Fig. 3.8. Linear algebra - comparison operators

Symbol [Operation Name]	Example of use
σ Sigma [Selection]	$\sigma_{Salary\geq 75000}(instructor)$
	Returns the rows of the input relation that satisfy the predicate
Π Pi[Projection]	$\pi_{(Id,Salary)}(instructor)$
	Return the output having selected attributes from all rows.
⋈ [Natural join]	***Instructor ⋈ department***
	Output pairs of rows from two input relations
X [Cartesian Product]	***instructor × department***
	Output all pairs of rows from the two input relations
U[Union]	***Πname (instructor) UΠname (student)***
	Output the union of tuples from the two input relations.

Fig. 3.9. Relational algebra basic operations

Id	Name	Dept_Name	Salary
10001	NBK Rao	Computer Science	125000
10456	Chowdhury	Electronics	98000
10234	Singh	Mathematics	69000
10999	Crick	Physics	65000
10333	Nike	History	23000
11002	Nina	Computer Science	28000

Fig. 3.10. A sample Instructor relation instance

Basic Operations

Selection Operation

Example:

Select the tuples of department name mathematics from the instructor relation

$$\sigma_{dept\_name="mathematics"}(instructor)$$

Select the tuples of salary less than 3the 0000 from the instructor relation

$$\sigma_{Salry<=30000}(instructor)$$

Projection Operation

It is a unary operation. Works on single relation and that returns argument relation.

List all attributes *ID*, *name*, and *salary from instructor relation.*

$$\pi_{(Id,name,Salary)}(instructor)$$

Composition of operations

Retrieve the faculty names in computer science department in instructor relation

$$\pi_{(name)}(\sigma_{dept\_name="computer\ science"}\ (instructor))$$

Union Operation

Retrieve the list of all courses taught in the even 2020 and odd 2021 semesters from section relation

$$\pi_{(courseid)}(\sigma_{semester==even \wedge year==2020}(section))\ U$$

$$\pi_{(name)}(\sigma_{semester="odd" \wedge year=2022}\ (Section))$$

Set Difference

Binary operation. It takes input as two relations. denoted by −. It gives the tuples which do not exist in the second relation and existed in the first relation.

The expression

r* – *s, gives an output relation having tuples in r not in s.

Example: Courses offered in even semester 2020 not in odd 2022.

$$\pi_{(courseid)}(\sigma_{semester="even" \wedge year=2020}(section))\ -$$

$$\pi_{(name)}(\sigma_{semester=odd \wedge year=2022}\ (Section))$$

Cartesian-Product Operation

The Cartesian product of relations *r* and s denoted as *r*× s. it used to combined at a from two relations.

Let A and B are two relations, then AXB will get the resultant relation as illustrated in Fig. 3.11 and 3.12.

Relation A

S_Name	Age	Sex	Dept
Nitu	18	F	CS
Sona	16	F	CS
Rim	20	M	ENG

Relation B

C_Id	Course	Dept
1	DSA	CS
2	DBMS	CS
3	English-1	ENG

A X B

S_Name	Age	Sex	Dept	C_Id	Course
Nitu	18	F	CS	1	DSA
Nitu	18	F	CS	2	DBMS
Nitu	18	F	ENG	3	English-1
Sona	16	F	CS	1	DS
Sona	16	F	CS	2	DBMS
Sona	16	F	ENG	3	English-1
Rim	20	M	CS	1	DS
Rim	20	M	CS	2	DBMS
Rim	20	M	ENG	3	English-1

Fig. 3.11. Relations A and B with sample data, and AXB resultant relation without projection and selection

$\sigma_{dept="CS"}(AXB)$

S_Name	Age	Sex	Dept	C_Id	Course
Nitu	18	F	CS	1	DSA
Nitu	18	F	CS	2	DBMS
Sona	16	F	CS	1	DS
Sona	16	F	CS	2	DBMS
Rim	20	M	CS	1	DS
Rim	20	M	CS	2	DBMS

$\pi_{Sname,course}\ \sigma_{dept="CS"}(AXB)$

S_Name	Course
Nitu	DSA
Nitu	DBMS
Sona	DS
Sona	DBMS
Rim	DS
Rim	DBMS

Fig. 3.12. Cartesian-Product Operation AXB resultant relation with selection and projection

Natural-Join Operation

It is a binary algebraic operation. It is symbolized with ⋈. The natural-join operation practices a Cartesian product of its two arguments and performs a selection by checking equality on those attributes that appear in both relations, and finally removes duplicate attributes.

Employee

Name	Id	Dept_name
A	120	IT
B	125	HR
C	110	Sale
D	111	IT

Department

Dept _name	Manager
Sale	Y
Prod	Z
IT	A

Employee ⋈ Department

Name	*Id*	*Dept_name*	*Manager*
A	120	IT	A
C	110	Sale	Y
D	111	IT	A

Fig. 3.13. The result of natural-join: Employee ⋈ Department

3.5. RELATIONAL CALCULUS

Relational calculus is implemented at two levels such as tuple and domain. These are non-procedural query languages.

3.5.1. TUPLE RELATIONAL CALCULUS (TRC)

A general representation of a TRC query is *{t | P(t)}*

Predicate in TRC:
Build with Logical components and quantifier
Logical - OR (V), AND (Λ), NOT(¬).
Quantifiers:
∃ - "there exists"
∀ - " for all"

Here, t - the set of tuples and P is apredicate

P(t) is true to generate all tuples in t.

P(t) conditions are

Logically combined with OR (V), AND (Λ),NOT(¬).

Quantifiers:

∃ - "there exists"

∃ t ∈ r (Q(t)) - 'there exists" a tuple t in relation r for predicate Q(t) is true.

∀ - " for all"

∀ t ∈ r (Q(t)) - Q(t) is true "for all" tuples t in relation r.

Example: Use TRC to select the facultyID, name, deptname, salary of faculty whose salary is more than 65,000/-.

{t | t ∈faculty Λt[salary] > 65000}

3.5.2. DOMAIN RELATIONAL CALCULUS (DRC)

Instead of using values for a complete tuple, the second type of relational calculus known as domain relational calculus employs domain variables that take values from the domain of an attribute. However, the domain relational calculus is intimately connected to the TRC.

A general form in the DRC is

{< x1, x2, . . . , xn > | P(x1, x2, . . . , xn)}

where x1, x2, . . . , xn represent domain variables. P signifies a formula of atoms, as was the case in the tuple relational calculus. An atom in the domain relational calculus has one of the following forms:

- $< x1, x2, x3, x4 \ldots\ldots, xn > \in r$, where r is a relation on n attributes and x1, x2, . . . , xn are domain variables or constants.
- x OP y, where x and y are domains and OP is a operator

$(<, \leq, =, \_=, >, \geq)$.

- x OP c, where x is a domain, OP is a comparison operator, and c is a

constant.

Example: Get the facultyID, name, deptname, and salary of faculty whose salary is more than 65000

<facultyID, fname, dept_name, and salary> domain attributes represented as <f, fn,dt,s>

$$\{< f, fn, dt, s > \mid < f, fn, dt, s > \in faculty \wedge s > 65000\}$$

Get all facultyIDs of faculty whose salary is more than 65000:

$$\{< f > \mid \exists f, d, s\ (< f, fn, dt, s > \in faculty \wedge s > 65000)\}$$

UNIT SUMMARY

- The logical level design of the system provided in relational modeling. Further this is helpful to the implementation at view level and physical level by using application programming languages.
- The conceptual design of the database system is provided in E-R and EER diagrams. Now this is mapped with relational model.
- In relational model:
  All entities are represented with tables
  Relationships are provided with
- Relational data model concepts:
  - Domain
  - Attribute
  - Relation
  - Database schema
  - Database instance
- Database constraints:
  - Implicit constraints
  - Explicit constraints
  - Semantic constraints
- The constraints on relational databases are implemented in four ways:
  - Domain
  - Key
  - Entity Integrity
  - Referential integrity
- Entity Relationship (E-R) model and Enhanced Entity Relationship (EER) model at conceptual design is mapped with the relational model at the logical level in three steps:
  Step 1: The entity sets with simple and complex attributes
  Step 2: Week entity sets
  Step 3: Relationship sets
- Relational algebra is a procedural query language. It defines a set of operations such as addition, subtraction, or multiplication.

- The operations in relational algebra are:

  Fundamental operations –project, select, union, Cartesian product, difference and rename

  Other operations - set intersection, natural join, and assignment.

- The fundamental operations are

  σ Sigma [Selection]

  Π Pi[Projection]

  ⋈ [Natural join]

  X [Cartesian Product]

  ∪[Union]

- Relational calculus:Tuple and Domain
- The general representation of a query in the TRC is denoted as:**{*t* | *P*(*t*)}**
- A general form in the DRC is

  {< x1, x2, . . . , xn > | P(x1, x2, . . . , xn)}

  where x1, x2, . . . , xn represent domain variables. P denotes a formula

EXERCISES

Multiple Choice Questions

1 DRC stands for
   a. Data Relational concepts
   b. Dependency Relational Calculus
   c. Domain Relational Calculus
   d. Domain Relational Concepts

2 In Relational Modeling, not related concept
   e. domain
   f. relation
   g. entity
   h. attribute

3 In logical design, the ER mapping of entity is
   a. constraints
   b. table
   c. attribute
   d. key attribute

4 The domain is not represented one of the following
   a. Name
   b. data type
   c. Constraint
   d. File

5 ....is not a component of a relational database.
   a. Entity
   b. Hierarchy
   c. Table
   d. Attribute

6 Inthe usage of DBMS, the vital one is to understand
   a. Physical schema
   b. All substances that the system supports
   c. One sub schema
   d. Both (A) and (B)

7 .... is not an implicit constraint in relational databases
   a. string
   b. primary
   c. integer
   d. float

8 .... is also called an explicit constraint in relational databases
   a. primary key
   b. referential integrity
   c. schema based integrity
   d. semantics

9 String is ....type of constraint in relational databases
   a. key constraint

b. referential integrity
c. domain constraint
d. unique constraint

10 Semantic constraints are implemented through……
a. key constraints
b. data definition language
c. data manipulation language
d. application programming language

11 Projection is ……….type of operation in relational algebra
a. binary
b. unary
c. more relations
d. trinity

12 _______produces the relation that has attributes of R1 and R2
a. Cartesian product
b. subtraction
c. Product
d. Intersection

13 Cartesian product in relational algebra is
a. Ternary
b. Binary
c. Unary
d. not

14 Predicate in relational calculus is constituted with………
e. raw facts
f. quantifiers
g. logical operators
h. C&D

15 The tuple relational calculus is proposed by
e. EF Codd
f. kahate
g. James Gossling
h. Dennies Rithchie

16 In the relational modes, cardinality is termed as:
a. No. of tuple's.
b. No. of attribute's.
c. No. of table's.
d. No. of constraint's

17 Relational calculus is a……………language
a. Procedural.
b. Non- Procedural
c. Data definition.
d. High level.

18 A relational database developer, a row is termed as
a. attribute
b. table
c. tuple
d. criteria

Answers to MCQs:

1	2	3	4	5	6	7	8	9	10	11	12	13	14	15	16	17	18
C	C	C	D	B	C	B	C	C	D	B	A	B	D	A	A	B	C

Short and Long Answer Type Questions

1. Summarise the steps in ER/EER model mapping in relational model.
2. Illustrate the basic structure of relational data model and label the all components.
3. Construct a logical design for a hospital management system with a set of patients and medical doctors. A patient log containsa history of tests conducted and consultations made.
4. List the different types of constraints with significant examples.
5. Identify three possible relations and related attributes that could be utilized to maintain the attributes of a social networking system like LinkedIn.
6. Outline the relational algebra operations with specific examples.
7. Identify three possible relations that could be utilized to store data in a social networking system like Facebook.

Numerical Problems

1.Build the subsequent queries in relational algebra, using the college schema.

a. List the offered courses in the Computer Science department having 4credits.

b. List the RollNos of enrolled students who were handled by afaculty name as Choudhary.

c. List the faculty having salary more than 50000.

2. Consider the employee database. Build queries in tuple relational calculus(TRC) and domain relational calculus(DRC):

a. Retrieve the employee names who are working for "DBS Bank".

b. Retrieve the employee names and their residence cities who work for "DBS Bank".

c. Retrieve the employee names, residence details of street addresses, and city who are working for "DBS Bank" and earning more than 50000.

PRACTICAL

1. A bank wants to automate each transaction. It provides the subsequent account types: Fixed Deposit(FD), Recurring Deposit(RD), and Savings Bank (SB)

The Bank also wants to monitor the loans granted to its clients. Identify the relations, attributes, datatypes and constraints.

Draw the relational schema diagramto provide all explicit constraints. Consider the following presumptions:

a. A customer is limited to having a single type of account. Joint accounts are not permitted

b. Only when a consumer has at least one of the account kinds is a loan available.

Use relational algebra for finding

a. account details of all fixed deposits

b. the account details of both fixed deposits and savings bank account

2. To represent the requirements of a small computer business corporation. Relational model with appropriate domain constraints

Relation 1 - The company workers assemble several computer models. Each employee's employee number, name, address, phone number, job title, and salary.

Relation 2 - The model, specifications, name, and quantity of each machine.

Relational instance - Each machine is made up of various components. The parts that are on hand must be listed in an inventory. A record of each part's name, cost, and available quantity is kept.

Relation 3 - These components are purchased from a number of providers. The supplier's name, address, and phone number must be kept on file.

use domain relational calculus:

retrieve the computer details that have been assembled are sold.

Commercial DB systems:

- IBM DB2 - www.ibm.com/software/data/db2
- Oracle - www.oracle.com
- Microsoft SQL Server - www.microsoft.com/sql
- Sybase - www.sybase.com
- IBM Informix - www.ibm.com/software/data/informix

Free/public domain database systems:

- MySQL - www.mysql.com
- PostgreSQL - www.postgresql.org

REFERENCES AND SUGGESTED READINGS

- Henry F Korth, Abraham Silberschatz, "Database system concepts", sixth ed., McGraw-Hill International editions, Computer Science Series
- Elmasri, Navathe, "Fundamentals of Database Systems", Elmasri, Navathe, Third ed, Addison Wesley
- Raghurama Krishnan, Johannes Gehrke, Database Management Systems, 3rd Edition, Tata McGraw Hill.
- C. J. Date, "An introduction to Database Systems", Sixth ed., Narosa Publications
- Database management systems- NPTEL: https://nptel.ac.in/courses/106105175

Dynamic QR Code for Further Reading

Relational Data Model
Relational Algebra Basic Operators
Relational Algebra Composition of Operators
Relational Algebra Additional Operators
Relational Algebra Extended Relational Algebra

https://nptel.ac.in/courses/106104135

4 STRUCTURED QUERY LANGUAGE(SQL)

UNIT SPECIFICS

Through this unit we have discussed the following aspects:

- *Structured Query Language (SQL-99)*
- *Schema definition*
- *Constraints, Queries, and Views*
- *Security; Introduction to SQL Programming Techniques*

The practical applications of the topics are discussed for working in real-time database environments such as commercial as well as open-source database management systems.

Besides giving a large number of multiple choice questions as well as questions of short and long answer types marked in two categories following the lower and higher order of Bloom's taxonomy, assignments through several numerical problems, a list of references, and suggested readings are given in the unit so that one can go through them for practice. It is important to note that for getting more information on various topics of interest some QR codes have been provided in different sections which can be scanned for relevant supportive knowledge.

After the related practical, based on the content, there is a "Know More" section. This section has been carefully designed so that the supplementary information provided in this part becomes beneficial for the users of the book. This section mainly highlights the initial activity, examples of some interesting facts, analogy, history of the development of the subject focusing on the salient observations and finding, timelines starting from the development of the concerned topics up to the recent time, applications of the subject matter for our day-to-day real life or/and industrial applications on a variety of aspects, case study related to environmental, sustainability, social and ethical issues whichever applicable, and finally inquisitiveness and curiosity topics of the unit.

RATIONALE

This structured query language unit on Database systems helps students to get knowledge on programming constructs and commands of SQL and its real-time applications. It provides a practical relational model using SQL standard for commercial relational DBMSs. It covers the programming language of SQL with more advanced features of the SQL language for relational databases including PL/SQL constructs. These constructs helps to users to create, retrieve and manage database with security.

SQL is an important aspect of commercial database systems that essentially deals with information and data and their effect on information retrieval. Structured query language (SQL) statements are started their journey by mathematical functions using calculus and algebra and then explaining it in terms of relational database management. This permits one to analyze the operations of many day-to-day transactions around us. Its practical applications are related to the relational model construction and operation of different types of database systems and tools.

PRE-REQUISITES

Mathematics: Calculus, Algebra (Class XII)
Computer Science: problem-solving with programming (Class XII)

UNIT OUTCOMES

The List of outcomes of this unit is as follows:

U4-O1: Summarize query language constructs and constraints to build database system.

U4-O1: Apply integrity constraints to guard traits and build database system.

U4-O2: Build queries to create, manage and retrieve data from database systems using commercial databases.

U4-O3: Create queries for efficient data retrieval by using SQL commands and clauses.

U4-O4: Use structured programming for providing security and authentication to the systems

Unit-4 Outcomes	EXPECTEDMAPPINGWITHSUBJECTOUTCOMES (1-Weak Correlation;2-Medium correlation;3-Strong Correlation)					
	CO-1	CO-2	CO-3	CO-4	CO-5	CO-6
U4-O1	3	1	3	-	-	-
U4-O2	1	1	1	-	-	-
U4-O3	2	2	3	-	-	-
U4-O4	3	3	3	-	-	-
U4-O5	3	3	3	-	-	-

4.1. STRUCTURED QUERY LANGUAGE (SQL-99)

SQL is a query language used to define the structure of the data, modify the data, and indicate the security constraints. SQL is expanded as a Structured Query Language, also called SEQUEL (Structured English QUEry Language). Initially, it was designed as an interface for the relational database system and implemented at IBM Research as a commercial relational DBMS.

> The standardization of SQL is by the American National Standards Institute (ANSI) and the International Standards Organization (ISO):::
> - The first SQL standard is called SQL-86 or SQL1
> - Expanded standard called SQL-92, or SQL2
> - The SQL:1999, which started out as SQL3
> - Additional updates to the standard are SQL: 2003 and SQL: 2006, which added XML features among other updates to the language.

Fig. 4.1 illustrates the various components of SQL. It includes Data definition language (DDL), transaction control language (TCL), and data manipulation language (DML), and data control language (DCL) are used to state and alter the database schema, and execute database queries, and update.

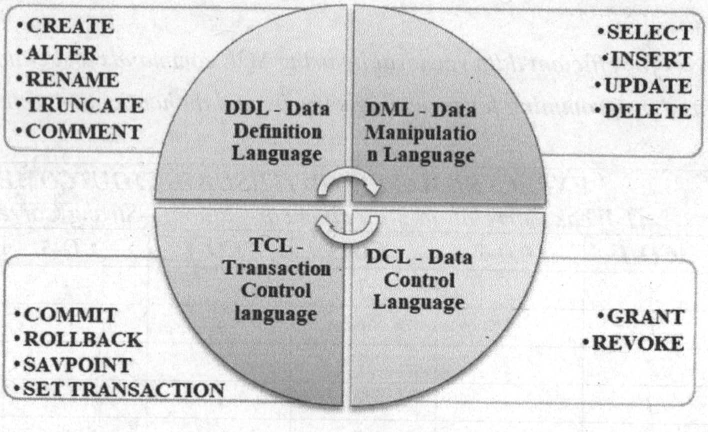

Fig. 4.1. Structured Query Language components

Fig. 4.2 shows the glossary of basic SQL commands.

CREATE - creates a new table/view

INSERT - inserts new data into a database

SELECT - extracts data from a database

UPDATE - updates data in a database

DELETE - deletes data from a database

ALTER - modifies the schema or view

DROP - deletes a table

RENAME – rename a table

COMMIT – buffer to a disk

ROLLBACK – rollback the changes made

GRANT – Assign privileges to users

REVOKE – remove the assigned privileges

Fig. 4.2. Glossary of basic SQL commands

4.2. SCHEMA DEFINITION

The relational model terms such as relation, tuples, and attributes are termed in SQL as terms table, rows, and columns respectively. The schema is recognized by a name; an identifier to indicate the user account (owner of the schema); in addition to that domain descriptors for each element in the schema. In general, the schema elements are table, view, data type, constraint, domain, and constructs that describe the schema.

In SQL, the *create table* statement creates a new table in database.

The general structure of create table statement is:
***create table** r* **(*C_1 D_1, C_2 D_2, ..., C_n D_n, IC_1, ..., IC_k*);**
*******r -> relation C→ Column/Attribute D→ Domain IC → Integrity***

Example:

```
create a branch relation.
Crete table branch
(bname char(18),
location char(20),
bud amount numeric(10,2),
```

In the schema of branch relation, 3 attributes – bname, location, and bud amount; the domains are a string of a maximum of 18 and 20 characters and numeric of a maximum of 10 digits of the total in which 2 are decimals; integrity constraint is a primary key attribute as bname. A semicolon indicates the end of the SQL statement.

In SQL, the *insert into* statement for inserting values to table in database.

The general structure of insert into statement is:
***Insert into** r*
*values(**V1, V2,V3,V4....Vn);***
*******r -> relation V→ Column/Attribute value***

A row inserted to table branch

Example:

```
Insert branch details to branch table
insert into branch values ('CSE. 'AB block'. '653298653'):
```

In SQL, the *select* statement for retrieving data values from table in database.

The general structure of select statement is:
***Select C1,C2,C3 from** r where <condition>;*
*******r -> relation C→ Column/Attribute, condition is a predicate on columns***

Example:

Extract all student details from table students

*Select * from students:*

Select rno, name, brach from students where branch='CSE';

In SQL, the *update* statement for changing data values in a table in database.

The general structure of update statement is:
***update** r set C1=newvalue where <condition>;;*
*******r -> relation C→ Column/Attribute Condition→ a predicate on columns***

SET clause is used to specify the change on attribute with new values.

Example:

update of student record rno 210 with new values marks 25 and contact no.

5555456790

update student **SET** smarks = 25, contact = 5555456790 **WHERE** Rno = 210;

In SQL, the *delete* statement for deleting data values in a table in database.

The general structure of delete statement is:
Delete from r where <condition>;
*******r -> relation Condition→ a predicate on columns***

Example:

delete student Roi record

delete from student WHERE Sname = 'Roi;

In SQL, the *alter* statement for modifying schema of table in database.

The general structure of alter table statement is:
***alter table** r drop column C1 cascade;*
*******r -> relation C→ Column/Attribute CASCADE is chosen, all constraints***
and views that reference the column are dropped automatically from the schema, along with the column.

Example:

alter table student, branch drop column roomno cascade;

Roomno column has been deleted from tables student, and branch

4.3. CONSTRAINTS

Constraints of the database are termed Integrity constraints, domain constraints, referential constraints, and data constraints.

4.3.1. INTEGRITY CONSTRAINTS:

The integrity constraints(IC) will protect the database from being accidentally damaged and ensure that the approved changes should not cause a data inconsistent.

Example:

Student registration number is unique to each.

The savings account balance should not be null.

Student age is not null.

Integrity constraints include primary key, foreign key, and not null.

Primary Key: Is having the property of not null and unique. It assures, the relation does not exist any tuples has a null value for a primary key attribute; and any two tuple values have the same value for a primary key attribute. A multicolumn (attribute) primary key is called a composite key.

The general form of adding primary key (create table at the end of attribute list):
***create table** r (A_1 D_1, A_2 D_2, ..., A_n D_n, primary key (A1 , A2 ,..., An));*

Example:

The dept attribute of the section relation should ensure not null and unique in all the tuples in the relation department.

create table dept(dname varchar(12), primary key (dname));

Foreign key: It establishes the relationship among tables. The values of attributes should assure any tuple in the relation must correspond to the values of the primary key attribute of some tuple in another relation.

The general form of adding primary key (create table at the end of attribute list):
create table r1 (A_1 D_1, A_2 D_2, ..., A_nD_n, foreign key (A1, A2,...,An)references r2);
******r2(A1, A2.....An) is a already created relation and having values.*

The foreign key should assure:

- If a similar value doesn't already exist in the primary key table, it rejects a value update or insert.
- If a delete would violate a references constraint, it would be rejected.
- Must refer to a unique column or primary key in the primary key table.
- The reference must be to a table, not a view or cluster.
- The reference column(s) and the foreign key column(s) have the same data types.

Example:

The dept attribute of the section relation should ensure the corresponding value existed in any of the tuples in the relation department.

The dept attribute of the section relation should ensure not null and unique in all the tuples in the relation department.

create table section(dept varchar(10), foreign key (dept) references department);

here department is existing relation having dept attribute as the primary key.

create table department(dept varchar(10), primary key (dept));

Not null: It does not allow a null value for that attribute.

Example:

The Faculty_name attribute of the faculty relation has not null constraint.

It ensures that the faculty_name of an instructor cannot be a null value.

4.3.2. DOMAIN CONSTRAINTS:

Domain constraints can be created along with attribute specification or using create a domain. Once a new domain is created, then we can refer data type with the created domain name.

The general form of create domain is:
Create Domain New Type As data type(length);

Create Domain reg_type As Char(10);

Here onwards reg_type can be used as a data type with char of length 10. Attributes like RNO, enrollmentID, reg_no data type are defined as reg_type.

Example:

Create an employee id data type with a name e_type of numeric data type of length 6 digit length. And use e_type for creating attributes of employeeid, mgr_id.

Crete domain e_type As numeric(6);

employeeid e_type;

mgr_id e_type;

4.3.3. DATA TYPES IN SQL:

The data types of SQL include numeric, character, bit, Boolean, date, and time.

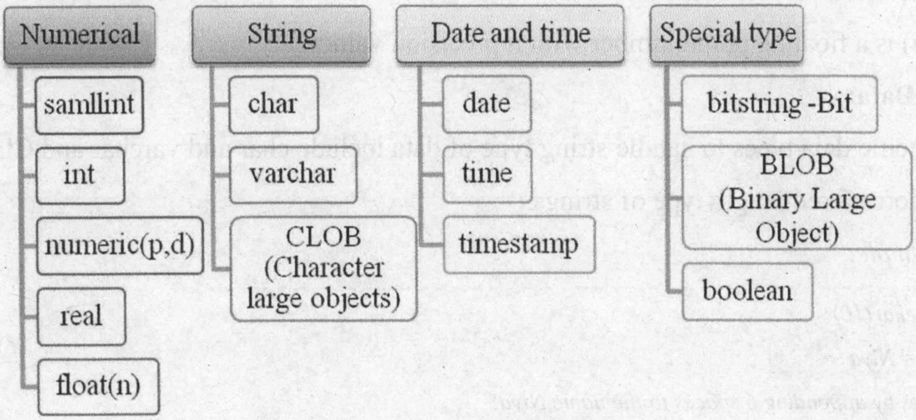

Fig. 4.3. Data types in SQL

Numerical data:

The specific data types include smallint, int, numeric, real, and float.

Integer or Int and smallint are a machine-dependent subsets of integers.

Example:

phone_no integer;

988776434

No decimal part is included in the value.

A numeric is a fixed point number with specific precision.

Denoted as *numeric(p,d)*

Example:

salary numeric(10,2);

98765432.98

10000000000.34

The salary attribute defines with a maximum of 10 digits and two precision values.

Real and double precision are types of floating point numbers whose precision levels depend on the machine.

Float(n) is a floating point number with n precision values.

String Data:

The specific data types to handle string type of data include char and varchar and CLOB

Char stores fixed-length type of strings.

Example:

Name char(10);

Name = Niya

It stores by appending 6 spaces to the name Niya.

Varchar:

Varchar data type stores variable-length strings.

Example:

Name varchar(10);

Name = Niya

It stores the name as Niya without any spaces(even though it is specified as a length of 10).

Comparison of char and varchar data types:

Char(n) – stores n characters. It stores total 10 characters by appending with spaces to the exact string.

If A=”Ani” and B=”Ani”

When doing string comparison (A=B) return false due to empty spaces.

Varchar(n) – stores maximum of n characters. It sores the exact characters without appending any empty spaces.

If A=”Ani” and B=”Ani”

When doing string comparison (A=B) return true.

CLOB (Character large objects): variable-length string data type. It is used to indicate the string values with a lot of text, or documents. You can specify the maximum CLOB length in kilobytes (K), megabytes (M), or gigabytes (G).

Example:

doc1 CLOB(30G) indicates a max. length of 30 gigabytes.

Data and Time data:

The specific data types to handle date and time includes the date, time, and timestamp.

DATE: It has ten positions including DAY, MONTH, and YEAR.

The general representation: DD-MM-YYYY.

Example:

DATE ‘2022-10-27’

TIME: It has at least eight positions and includes HOUR, MINUTE, and SECOND. The general form of representation: HH:MM:SS

Example:

```
TIME '08:11:57'
```

Timestamp: It includes both the DATE and TIME fields, along with a min. of six fractions of seconds and an optional TIME ZONE.

Example:

```
TIMESTAMP '2022-10-28 08:11:57.346312
```

Other types of data:

Bitstring:

BIT(n) - A fixed length of a maximum number of bits n

BIT VARYING(n), a varying length of a max. no. of n bits.

Example:

```
bstring BIT(5);
bstring = B '10101' ( the value should be preceded by the letter B)
```

BLOB - BINARY LARGE OBJECT

It is a variable-length bitstring and used for large binary values such as image data.

Boolean:

In general, it holds the binary value TRUE or FALSE. In SQL, a tri value UNKNOWN, TRUE and FALSE.

4.3.4. ATTRIBUTE CONSTRAINTS AND DEFAULTS

NOT NULL constraint: SQL allows NULL values to the attributes. A null value is not equivalent to a value of zero. A column becomes a required column when its name is defined as not null. Any expression that contains a null value will also return null. For instance, 30 times null results in null.

UNIQUE key constraint: used to make sure that each record's column of data has unique information. More than one unique key may be present in a table.

Example:

The license number of the vehicle is unique.

Create table employee_details (customer_id numeric(8) primary key, employee_name varchar(20) not null, employee_address varcher (25) not null, license_number varchar (15) constraint unique);

DEFAULT clause: used to define a value as a default value to the attribute.

Example:

Create an employee schema with details of contact number, and marital status.

create table employee (employee_id number(5), employee_name varchar(20) not null, contact_no varchar(10), marital_status char(1) default 'M' , primary key (employee id));

CHECK clause: used to restrict the specified constraint and default values to the attributes.

Example:

```
contact integer(10) not null;
Balance numeric(10,2)not null default 2000;
bnumber integer not null check (bnumber > 0 AND bnumber < 15);
check (DOJ <= DOL);
```

Create a table of an employee where the Employee_Id column should start with 'M' and the city is one among the list as 'Hyderabad, 'Chennai, 'Odisha, 'Karnataka..

```
SQL> create table employee_details
(employee_id numeric(8) constraint ck_ecode check (employee_id like 'M%),
employee_name varchar(20) not null,
City varchar(25) constraint ck_city check (the city in 'Hyderabad, 'Chennai, 'Odisha,
'Karnataka),
salary numeric(5), primary key (employee_id));
```

4.3.5. CASE STUDY – COLLEGE DATABASE

*An example system would be a **College database** that would be used to maintain information regarding major entities such as student, branch, course, and grade in a college. Initially, the college database is set up with five tables having identical data records.*

STUDENT file contains information about each student;

COURSE file contains information about each course;

SECTION file contains information about all sections of a course;

BRANCH file contains information about individual departments in the college;

FACULTY_COURSEWORK file contains information about each faculty taught courses.

The table creation with appropriate integrity constraints of the college database is as follows::::

Relation: Branch/department	**Relation: Subject**
create table branch(branch_name varchar(10), Title varchar(15), location varchar(5), budget numeric(10,2), **primary key**(branch_name));	create table Subject(Subject_Id varchar(7), title varchar(50), branch_name varchar(20), credits integer(2), primary key(Subject_Id), foreign key (branch_name));
Relation: Faculty/Instructor	**Relation: Section**
create table faculty (faculty_Id integer(5), name varchar(15), salary numeric (8,2), primary key (faculty_Id), foreign key (branch_ name) references branch);	**create table** section (Subject_Id varchar(7), Section_Id varchar(5), semester varchar(6), year numeric(4,0), building varchar(15), room_no varchar(7), slot varchar(4), primary key (Subject_Id, Section _Id, semester, year), foreign key (Subject_Id) references Subject);
Relation: Faculty_Subject work	**Relation: Student**
create table faculty_teaches (faculty_Id varchar(5), Subject_Id varchar(8), section_Id varchar(8), semester varchar(6), year numeric(4,0), primary key (faculty_Id, Subject_Id, section_Id, semester, year), foreign key (Subject_Id, section_Id, semester, year) references section, foreign key (faculty_Id) references	create table student(Roll_No integer(6), Student_name varchar(15), branch_name varchar(10), Subject_Id varchar(8), primary key(Roll_No), foreign key(branch_name) references branch, foreign key (Subject_Id) references Subject);

Fig. 4.4. SQL data definition of the college database

4.3.6. CASE STUDY – LIBRARY MANAGEMENT SYSTEM

An example system would be a Library Management System having the following factors are taken into account while tracking readers in the database:

A single point authentication system that consists of a login ID and password, the system maintains the track of the staff logs.

The library staff updates the book collection with information on each title's ISBN, price in Indian rupees, category types (general, innovations, story), edition number, and unique author number.

A publisher has a publisher ID number, the booktitle, and the year it was published.

Member register by providing a member ID, MailId, member name (firstname and lastname), contact number (multiple numbers are permitted), and contact address. The library staff monitor the readers.

Books that have the issue and return date stamped can be considered as reserved by readers. It can have a due date as well if it is not returned within the allotted time frame.

The table creation with appropriate integrity constraints of a library management system is as follows::::

Relation: Book	**Relation: Member**
create table Book(Book_Id integer(5), auther_no integer(5), ISBN_no varchar(10), Title varchar(15), edition_no integer(4), category_type varchar(5), price numeric(10,2), **primary key**(ISBN_no));	**create table member**(member_Id integer(5), mail_Id varchar(15), address varchar(20), Contact_no integer(10), Mem_name varchar(15), **primary key**(member_id));
Relation: Publisher	**Relation: Authentication**
create table Publisher_details (Publisher_Id integer(5), YOP integer(4), Book_title varchar(15), **primary key**(Publisher_ID));	**create table** Authentication (Login_Id varchar(15), PSW varchar(15), **primary key**(Login_ID));
Relation: Staff	***Relation: reserve/return***
create table Lib_Staff (staff_id integer(7), Name varchar(15), **primary key**(staff_id));	**create table** Reserve_Return(book_id integer(5), member_id integer(5), Resdate date, Duedate date, Retdate date, foreign key(book_id) references book, foreign key(member_id) references member);

Fig. 4.5. SQL data definition of the library management system database

4.4. QUERIES

4.4.1. BASIC STRUCTURE OF QUERY

The basic structure of SQL retrieval query is **select-from-where** block.

```
SELECT <attribute list>
FROM <table list>
WHERE <condition>;
```

<attribute list> -> list of attribute names whose values are to be retrieved by the query

<table list> list of the relation names required to process the query.

<condition> A conditional phrase that identify the tuples to be retrieve by the query.

Select – project - condition

Query-0: Retrieve the DOB and residence of the student whose name is 'Rai C. Roy'.

Q-0: select DOB, residence from students where Firstname = 'Rai' and Middlename = 'C' and Lastname = 'Roy';

Select - all attributes - condition

Q1: Retrieve the student details of who enrolled in CSE.

Q1: select * from students where branch='CSE';

Select - <multiple tables> - project

Q2. Retrieve the Emp_name and salary of all employees who work for the 'sales' department.

Q2: select Firstname, Lastname, Residence from employee, branch where Bname = 'sales';

Natural Join: It operates on two tables and produces a table as the result. It considers the pairs of tuples having both attributes in both tables with the same value.

Inner Join - returns the identical rows from both the tables.

Outer Join- performed in three ways - Left, Right, and Full outer joins

Example:

All faculty, who teaches some Subject in the college, find their names and the Subject_IDs of all Subjects they taught.

select faculty_name, Subject_id from faculty, teach where faculty.ID= teach.ID;

Using Join: select-project-join

Example:

select faculty_name, Subject_id from faculty natural join teach;

Without using join(Cartesian Product):

Retrieve the project_id, the managing dept_id, and the department head's name, address, and DOB of every project located in 'Delhi'.

Q3: select Pnumber, Dnum, Lname, Address, Bdate from project, department, employee where D_num = D_no and Head_ID = ID and P_location = 'Delhi';

4.4.2. ADDITIONAL BASIC OPERATIONS

Rename:

Renaming of the attribute is performed using *as* a clause. The *as* clause can be used in both the *select* and *from* clauses.

General representation:

Old column name as new column name

Column renaming:

All faculty in the college who taught some Subject, list their names and the Subject ID of all Subjects they taught.

select *facuty_name as Subject faculty*, Subject_id from faculty, teach where faculty.faculty_ID = teach.t_ID;

Table renaming: table name referred with alias name using as clause

List the name of all faculty whose salary is more than at least one faculty in the CSE department

select distinct F.faculty_name from Faculty as F, Faculty as CS where F.salary > CS.salary and CS.dept name = 'CSE';

STRING OPERATIONS

SQL provides various string-handling functions on character strings:

1. Concatenating (use symbol "||")
2. extract sub-strings
3. Find the string length
4. Convert strings to uppercase (use upper(s) where s is a string) and lowercase (use lower(s))
5. Remove spaces at the end of the string (using trim(s))

Function	Description
CONCAT	Adds two or more expressions together
CONCAT_WS	Adds two or more expressions together with a separator
FIELD	Returns the index position of a value in a list of values
FIND_IN_SET	Returns the position of a string within a list of strings
FORMAT	Formats a number to a format like "#,###,###.##", rounded to a specified number of decimal places
INSERT	Inserts a string within a string at the specified position and for a certain number of characters
INSTR	Returns the position of the first occurrence of a string in another string
LCASE	Converts a string to lower-case
LEFT	Extracts a number of characters from a string (starting from left)
LENGTH	Returns the length of a string (in bytes)
LOCATE	Returns the position of the first occurrence of a substring in a string
LOWER	Converts a string to lower-case
LPAD	Left-pads a string with another string, to a certain length
LTRIM	Removes leading spaces from a string
MID	Extracts a substring from a string (starting at any position)
POSITION	Returns the position of the first occurrence of a substring in a string
REPEAT	Repeats a string as many times as specified
REPLACE	Replaces all occurrences of a substring within a string, with a new substring
REVERSE	Reverses a string and returns the result
RIGHT	Extracts a number of characters from a string (starting from right)
RPAD	Right-pads a string with another string, to a certain length
RTRIM	Removes trailing spaces from a string
SPACE	Returns a string of the specified number of space characters
STRCMP	Compares two strings
SUBSTR/ SUBSTRING	Extracts a substring from a string (starting at any position)
SUBSTRING_INDEX	Returns a substring of a string before a specified number of delimiter occurs
TRIM	Removes leading and trailing spaces from a string
UCASE/UPPER	Converts a string to upper-case

Fig. 4.6. MySQL functions of string operations

Pattern matching: It is performed on strings, using the operator *like* and two special characters (% and _):

Percent (%): The % characters match any substring.

Underscore (_): The character match any character.

Examples: Pattern string with special characters

'Intro%' matches a string beginning with "Intro".

'%put%' matches a sub string "put" as a substring, for example, 'Intro. to Computer Science', and 'Computational Biology'.

' --- ' matches any string of exactly three characters.

' ---%' matches any string of at least three characters.

'\' escape character to match the special character in string

Example: *Pattern matching using like operator and string with special characters*

like 'xy\%zr%' - '\ ' matches all strings beginning with "xy%zr".

like 'xy\\z%' escape '\ ' matches all strings beginning with "xy\z".

SQL AGGREGATE OPERATORS

1. **Count**: It provides a tuple's count in that column. If a DISTINCT keyword is used then it will return only the count of a unique tuple in the column. Otherwise, it will return a count of all the tuples (including duplicates) count (*) indicates all the tuples of the column.
2. **SUM**: It provides the sum of all the values in that column. If a DISTINCT keyword is used then it will return the sum of all unique values in the columns.
3. **AVG**: It provides the average value of that column values. If a DISTINCT keyword is used then it will return the average of distinct values only.
4. **MAX**: It provides the highest value of that column.
5. **MIN**: It provides the lowest value of that column.

Function	Description
ABS	Returns the absolute value of a number
ACOS	Returns the arc cosine of a number
ASIN	Returns the arc sine of a number
ATAN	Returns the arc tangent of one or two numbers
ATAN2	Returns the arc tangent of two numbers
AVG	Returns the average value of an expression
CEIL	Returns the smallest integer value that is >= to a number
CEILING	Returns the smallest integer value that is >= to a number
COS	Returns the cosine of a number
COT	Returns the cotangent of a number
COUNT	Returns the number of records returned by a select query
DEGREES	Converts a value in radians to degrees
DIV	Used for integer division
EXP	Returns e raised to the power of a specified number
FLOOR	Returns the largest integer value that is <= to a number
GREATEST	Returns the greatest value of the list of arguments
LEAST	Returns the smallest value of the list of arguments
LN	Returns the natural logarithm of a number
LOG	Returns the natural logarithm of a number, or the logarithm of a number to a specified base
LOG10	Returns the natural logarithm of a number to base 10
LOG2	Returns the natural logarithm of a number to base 2
MAX	Returns the maximum value in a set of values
MIN	Returns the minimum value in a set of values
MOD	Returns the remainder of a number divided by another number
PI	Returns the value of PI
POW	Returns the value of a number raised to the power of another number
POWER	Returns the value of a number raised to the power of another number
RADIANS	Converts a degree value into radians
RAND	Returns a random number
ROUND	Rounds a number to a specified number of decimal places
SIGN	Returns the sign of a number
SIN	Returns the sine of a number
SQRT	Returns the square root of a number
SUM	Calculates the sum of a set of values
TAN	Returns the tangent of a number
TRUNCATE	Truncates a number to the specified number of decimal places

Fig. 4.7. MySQL functions of aggregate operations

SET OPERATIONS

SQL supports set operations over two relations to construct queries such as union, intersect, and except.

Union

Example:

List all subjects offered either in even 2009 or in odd 2010, or both.

(select *Subject_id* **from** *section* **where** *semester* = 'odd' **and** *year*= 2021)
union
(select *Subject_ id* **from** *section* **where** *semester* = 'even' **and** *year*= 2022);

Intersect

Example:

List all Subjects taught in the odd 2021 as well as in even 2022.

(**select** Subject_id **from** section **where** *semester* = 'odd' **and** *year*= 2021)
intersect
(**select** Subject_id **from** section **where** *semester* ='even' **and** *year*= 2022);

Except Operation

The except performs set difference. It outputs all rows from its first relation that does not occur in the second relation.

Example:

List all Subjects taught in the odd 2021 but not in even 2022.

(select *Subject_ id* from *section* where *semester* = 'odd' and *year*= 2021)
except
(select *Subject_id* from *section* where *semester* ='even' and *year*= 2022);

IN /NOT IN

in / not in constrains for performing the tests on the set along with select.

Example:

List all Subjects offered in 2021 and 2022.

select *Subject_ id* from *section* where year in ('2021', 2022');

List all Subjects not offered in 2021 and 2022.

select *Subject_ id* from *section* where year not in ('2021', 2022');

>some / > all

SQL provides comparisons like >some, >=some, <some, <=some, =some, and <> some

- = **some** is identical to **in** and <> **some** is identical to **not in.**
- some is used to represent the phrase 'greater than at least one'

- >all is used to represent the 'greater than all'
- SQL provides comparisons like <all, <=all, >all, >=all <>all, =all.

Complex Queries:

Complex queries are not possible to write in a single SQL block. Two ways to compose a complex query in multiple SQL blocks.

Derived relations - SQL allows a sub-query expression to be used in the *from* clause.

Example:

Find the average salary of those branches where the average salary is greater than 65000/-

select B_name, avg (salary) ***from (select B_name, avg(salary) from faculty group by B_name) as*** *Branch_avg_sal (B_name,avg(salary))* ***where*** *Avg_salary > 65000;*

Find the maximum salary across all branches total salary at each branch.

select max (Tot_salary)
from ***(select B_name, sum(salary) from faculty group by B_name)*** *as branch_total (B_name, Tot_salary);*

With clause - provides a temporary view and is available in a query.

Aggregation with Grouping

group by clause

Example:

List the average salary in each department.

select *dept_ name*, **avg** (*salary_amt*) **as** *avg_salary* **from** *faculty* **group by** *dept_ name;*

having clause – followed by group by clause to perform grouping by condition

4.5. VIEWS

SQL views provide a virtual table, which is dynamically constructed for a user-specific by extracting data from base table(s). It is a custom-made representation of the data contained in one or more table(s) / view(s). It takes the output of a query and creates a table; therefore, it is a stored query or a virtual table. It provides further security to the tables by restricting access to the existing data from a table. It provides a simplified query structure to the user and hides the data complexity.

Why views:

- To simplify queries
- Similar to the queried from a base table
- Gives extended data security

Create - view

The general form to create a view:
create view view name as
select **column name, column name** from **table name** where **column name = expression list;**

Example:

Create a view with attributes book_title, and author_name on Book relation

```
create view V_Book as select book_title, author_name from book;
```

updating a view:

In general, views are readable. To perform data manipulation at views it should pass to the respective table.

To make views updatable, they should meet the following criterion:

- Only one table may be used to generate it.
- The view needs to contain the table's primary key column.
- The select statement does not allow the use of aggregate functions.
- A Distinct, Group by, or Having clause should not be present in the select statement used to create a view.

- Subqueries should not be utilized in the select statement used to create a view.
- It can't employ value expressions like total / 5 or constants, strings, or constants.

Example:

Retrieve data from view - *List all the titles of books written by author 'Sanjay.*

select book_title from V_book where book_title = 'Sanjay';

Dropping a view - *delete a view V_Book*

Drop view V_Book

4.6. SECURITY

Assigning a user's privileges to parts of the database is called authorization. Authorizations on data may contain reading, inserting new data, updating data, and deleting data.

Granting or revoking

SQL data definition language (DDL) provides a set of commands like grant, revoke to confer, and revoke privileges. The grant statement is used to confer authorization.

The general form of grant statement is:
grant <privileges list>
on <table or view >
to <user list>;

To revoke an authorization, SQL provides a **revoke** keyword.

The general form of revoke statement is:
revoke <privileges list>
on <table or view >
to <user list>;

The SQL provides the privileges of select, insert, update, and delete. The privilege type *'all privileges'* can be used for all the allowable privileges.

Example:

Example: Give authorization to Mr. Roi and Head_est for an update on the salary attribute of the salary_master relation:

grant update (salary) on salary_master to Roi, head_est;

remove update privilege from rai on salary master table

revoke update (salary) on salary_master to Roi, head_est;

4.7. INTRODUCTION TO SQL PROGRAMMING TECHNIQUES

The PL/SQL programming language as a procedural extension language for SQL was developed by Oracle Corporation in the late 1980s available as an Oracle database. PL/SQL offers a built-in, interpreted, and OS-independent programming environment. And it can be called from the command-line SQL*Plus interface. It is a fully portable, high-performance transaction processing language.

Features of PL/SQL programming:

- Close integration with SQL
- Thorough error checking.
- A wide variety of programming structures and data types.
- Supports object-oriented programming and structured programming through functions and procedures.

Advantages of PL/SQL:

- SQL is the industry-standard database language, and PL/SQL and SQL are tightly interconnected.
- Both static and dynamic SQL are supported by PL/SQL.
- DML operations and transaction control from PL/SQL blocks are supported using static SQL. PL/SQL blocks can contain DDL statements when using Dynamic SQL.

- PL/SQL enables batching of statements to be sent to the database. This lowers network traffic and gives the applications exceptional performance.
- PL/SQL allows programmers to query, manipulate, and update data in a database, due to this it increases programmers' productivity.
- Strong features like exception handling, encapsulation, data hiding, and object-oriented data types in PL/SQL reduce design and debugging time.
- PL/SQL applications are completely portable.
- It offers a high level of security.
- Access to preconFig.d SQL packages is provided.
- It offers assistance in Object-Oriented Programming for creating Server Page's and Web Applications.

4.7.1. STRUCTURE OF PL SQL BLOCK:

Block-based programming is used to structure the code in PL/SQL. An anonymous block is one that lacks a name not saved in oracle database. It is the most basic PL/SQL unit and helpful for building test units and is only used once. The declaration, execution, and exception handling are three fundamental parts. The other sections are optional; just the execution portion is required.

The illustration of anonymous block syntax:

```
[DECLARE]
Declaration statements;
BEGIN
Execution statements;
[EXCEPTION]
Exception handling statements;
END;
```

Declaration section - Used to specify variables, structures, and data types. Give names, data types, and starting values when declaring variables.

Execution section - Used to insert code or logic into block structures; at least one statement is required. It starts with the term BEGIN. The execution portion contains both procedural and SQL statements.

Exception section: Used to handle exceptions through either catch or handle.

Example:

To create Pl/SQL block which inserts 2 records in the student table?

```
BEGIN
insert into student_details values('R104','Roi', 21);
insert into student_details values('R105','Nitu',18);
END;
```

Named Block:

A named block is a specific kind of block that begins with the header section, which identifies the block's name and kind. These come in two varieties: procedures and functions.

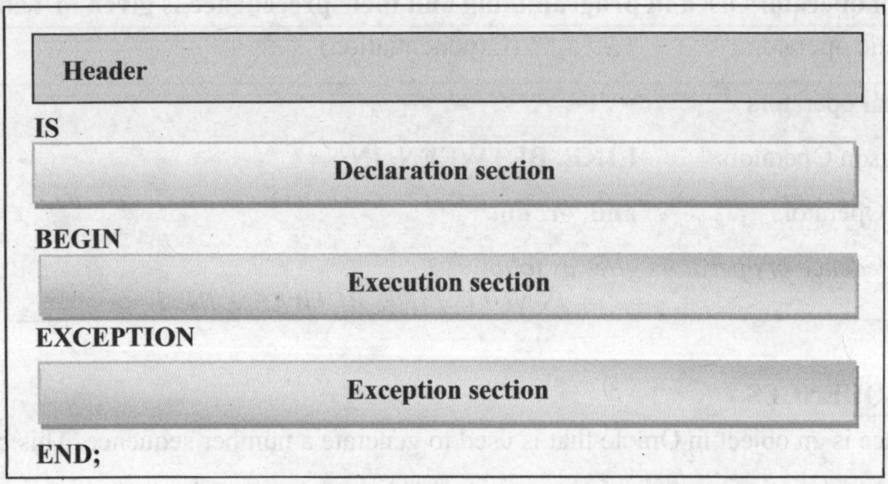

Fig. 4.8. General block structure of PL/SQL

Header - Used for named blocks. Which are called by name, parameter list, and return clause (for functions)

Generate output from - DBMS_OUTPUT is a built_in package that is used to display the output, and debugging information, and send messages from PL/SQL blocks, subprograms, packages, and triggers.

Example:

Display a hello message using put_line

```
BEGIN
dbms_output.put_line('Hello');
dbms_output.put_line('Welcome');
END;
```

Output: Hello
World
Welcome

4.7.2. PL/SQL – OPERATORS

The list of operators used in programming and their precedence is given in Table.

Arithmetic operators	+,-,*,/,** (Exponentiation)
Relational operators	= , !=, >, <, <=, >=
Comparison Operators	**LIKE, BETWEEN, IN**
Logical Operators	**and, or, not**

The precedence of operators goes as follows:
=, <, >, <=, >=, <>, !=, ~=, ^=, IS NULL, LIKE, BETWEEN, IN.

4.7.3. SEQUENCES

A sequence is an object in Oracle that is used to generate a number sequence. This can be useful when you need to create a unique number to act as a primary key.

Create Sequence:

The structure to create a sequence is:

```
CREATE SEQUENCE seq_name
INVALUE value
      MAXVALUE value
      START WITH value
      INCREMENT BY value
      CACHE value;
```

Example:

create a sequence strtas at 5 and ends at 199.

```
CREATE SEQUENCE five_seq
MINVALUE 5
MAXVALUE 199
START WITH 5
INCREMENT BY 1
CACHE 20;
```

DROP sequence

```
DROP SEQUENCE sequence_name
```

Example:

```
DROP SEQUENCE five_seq;
```

4.7.4. PL/SQL CONTROL STRUCTURES

Testing Conditions: IF and CASE Statements. There are three forms of IF statements:

IF-THEN; IF-THEN-ELSE, and IF-THEN-ELSIF

Example:

Demo of a simple IF-THEN Statement

```
DECLARE
performance NUMBER(8,2) := 1010
base NUMBER(8,2) := 10000;
increment NUMBER(6,2);
fid NUMBER(6) := 120;
BEGIN
IF performance > (base + 200) THEN
increment:= (sales - quota)/4;
UPDATE employees SET salary = salary + increment WHERE emp_id = fid_id;
END IF;
END;
/
```

A demo on case-when statement

```
DECLARE
gradepoint CHAR(1);
BEGIN
gradepoint := 'B';
CASE gradepoint
WHEN 'A' THEN DBMS_OUTPUT.PUT_LINE('Excellent');
WHEN 'B' THEN DBMS_OUTPUT.PUT_LINE('Very fair');
WHEN 'C' THEN DBMS_OUTPUT.PUT_LINE('fair);
WHEN 'D' THEN DBMS_OUTPUT.PUT_LINE('good');
WHEN 'F' THEN DBMS_OUTPUT.PUT_LINE('fail');
ELSE DBMS_OUTPUT.PUT_LINE('No grade');
END CASE;
END;
```

LOOP- END LOOP – control statement

The general form:

```
LOOP
sequence_of_statements
END LOOP;
```

EXIT-WHEN

EXIT– unconditionally stops the iterations.

WHEN conditionally stop the loops.

FOR-LOOP

Example:

```
A demo on for loop
DECLARE
n NUMBER := 0;
BEGIN
FOR r IN 1..100 LOOP — generate a sequence of 100 terms
n := n + (r**2);
END LOOP;
DBMS_OUTPUT.PUT_LINE( 'sum of sequence : ' || n );
END;
```

4.7.5. CURSORS

A **cursor** is a pointer to the context area. A cursor holds the rows (one or more) returned by a SQL statement. The set of rows the cursor holds is referred to as the **active set**. There are two types of cursors "

- Implicit cursors
- Explicit cursors

Implicit cursors - automatically created by Oracle whenever an SQL statement is executed, when there is no explicit cursor for the statement. Whenever a DML statement (INSERT, UPDATE, and DELETE) is issued, an implicit cursor is associated with this statement. For INSERT operations, the cursor holds the data that needs to be inserted. For UPDATE and DELETE operations, the cursor identifies the rows that would be affected. In PL/SQL, the most recent implicit cursor, always has attributes such as %FOUND, %ISOPEN, %NOTFOUND, and %ROWCOUNT.

Attribute	Returns
%FOUND	TRUE if an INSERT, UPDATE, or DELETE statement affected one or more rows or a SELECT statement returned one or more rows. Else FALSE
%NOTFOUND	TRUE if an INSERT, UPDATE, or DELETE statement affected no rows, or a SELECT statement returned no rows.
%ISOPEN	FALSE for implicit cursors
%ROWCOUNT	The number of rows affected by an INSERT, UPDATE, or DELETE statement, or returned by a SELECT statement.

Example:

illustration of cursor, that will update the table and increase the salary of each faculty by 5000 and use the SQL%ROWCOUNT attribute to determine the number of rows affected.

```
DECLARE
no_row number(2);
BEGIN
UPDATE faculty
SET salary = salary + 5000;
IF sql%notfound THEN
dbms_output.put_line('no facylty selected');
ELSIF sql%found THEN
no_row := sql%rowcount;
dbms_output.put_line( total_rows || 'facylty selected');
END IF;
END;
/
```

Explicit Cursors:

Explicit cursors are programmer-defined cursors for gaining more control over the context area. An explicit cursor should be defined in the declaration section of the

PL/SQL Block. It is created on a SELECT Statement which returns more than one row.

The general form of creating explicit cursor is:
CURSOR cursor_name IS select_statement;

Working with an explicit cursor includes the following steps:

- Declaring the cursor for initializing the memory
- Opening the cursor for allocating the memory
- Fetching the cursor for retrieving the data
- Closing the cursor to release the allocated memory

Cursor operation	Example
Declaration	CURSOR c_student IS SELECT rno, name, address FROM student;
Open	OPEN c_student;
Fetch	FETCH c_student INTO c_id, c_name, c_addr;
Close	CLOSE c_student;

Example

illustration of explicit cursor

```
DECLARE
s_id students.id%type;
s_name students.No.ame%type;
s_addr students.address%type;

CURSOR c_ students is
SELECT id, name, address FROM students;
BEGIN
OPEN c_ students;
LOOP
FETCH c_ students into c_id, c_name, c_addr;
EXIT WHEN c  students %notfound;
```

4.7.6. TRANSACTIONS

A database **transaction** is an atomic unit of work that may consist of one or more related SQL statements.

Transaction operation	Description
COMMIT	A transaction is made permanent by issuing the SQL command ***COMMIT***.
ROLLBACK	Changes made to the database without COMMIT could be undone using the ROLLBACK command. ***ROLLBACK [TO SAVEPOINT < savepoint_name>];***
SAVEPOINT	Savepoints are sort of markers that help in splitting a long transaction into smaller units by setting some checkpoints. ***SAVEPOINT < savepoint_name >;***

Example:

Illustration of the transaction on emp table.

```
INSERT INTO EMP (EID,ENAME, AGE, E_ADDRESS, SALARY)
VALUES (12, 'Roi, 39, 'LP', 19500 );
INSERT INTO EMP (EID, ENAME, AGE, E_ADDRESS, SALARY)
VALUES (18, 'Rini, 25, 'Wall', 55000 );
SAVEPOINT save1;
UPDATE EMP
SET SALARY = SALARY + 10000;
ROLLBACK TO save1;
UPDATE EMP
SET SALARY = SALARY + 10000
WHERE ID = 18;
UPDATE EMP
SET SALARY = SALARY + 5000
WHERE ID = 12;
COMMIT;
```

****** ROLLBACK TO save1: rolls back all the changes up to the point, where you had marked savepoint save1.*

SET AUTOCOMMIT ON;

When an environment variable is set on, then execute commit automatically after inserting, updating, and deleting.

4.7.7. PROCEDURES AND FUNCTIONS

A subprogram is a program unit/ module that performs a specific task. PL/SQL subprograms are named PL/SQL blocks that can be invoked with a set of parameters. PL/SQL provides two kinds of subprograms

Functions - return a single value; mainly used to compute and return a value.

Procedures - do not return a value directly; mainly used to act.

```
The general form of creating a procedure:
CREATE [OR REPLACE] PROCEDURE procedure_name
[(parameter_name [IN | OUT | IN OUT] type [, ...])]
{IS | AS}
BEGIN
< procedure_body >
END procedure_name;
```

Parameter mode	Description
IN	passes a value to the subprogram. It is a read-only parameter.
OUT	returns a value to the calling program. It acts like a variable.
IN OUT	passes an initial value to a subprogram and returns an updated value to the caller. It can be assigned a value and the value can be read.

FUNCTIONS

The general form of creating a function:

```
CREATE [OR REPLACE] FUNCTION function_name
[(parameter_name [IN | OUT | IN OUT] type [, ...])] RETURN
return_datatype
{IS | AS}
BEGIN
< function_body >
```

Example:

Illustration of creating a function.

```
CREATE OR REPLACE FUNCTION total faculty
RETURN number IS
total_faculty number(2) := 0;
BEGIN
SELECT count(*) into total_faculty
FROM faculty;
RETURN total_faculty;
END;
/
```

Illustration of calling a PL/SQL function.

```
DECLARE
cf number(2);
BEGIN
cf := total faculty();
dbms_output.put_line('Total no. of Faculty: ' || cf);
END;
/
```

4.7.8. EXCEPTIONS HANDLING

An exception is an error condition during program execution. PL/SQL supports programmers to catch such conditions using the **EXCEPTION** block in the program and appropriate action is taken against the error condition. There are two types of exceptions

- System-defined exceptions
- User-defined exceptions

```
The general form of handling exception handling:
DECLARE
<declarations section>
BEGIN
<executable command(s)>
EXCEPTION
<exception handling goes here >
WHEN exception1 THEN
exception1-handling-statements
WHEN exception2 THEN
exception2-handling-statements
WHEN exception3 THEN
exception3-handling-statements
WHEN others THEN
exception3-handling-statements
END;
END [function_name];
```

Example:

Illustration of exception handling on employee table.

```
DECLARE
e_id employee.id%type := 8;
e_name employee.Name%type;
e_addr employee.address%type;
BEGIN
SELECT name, address INTO e_name, e_addr FROM employee WHERE id = e_id;
DBMS_OUTPUT.PUT_LINE ('Name: '|| e_name);
DBMS_OUTPUT.PUT_LINE ('Address: ' || e_addr);
EXCEPTION
WHEN no_data_found THEN
dbms_output.put_line('No such employee!');
WHEN others THEN
dbms_output.put_line('Error!');
END;
```

4.7.9. TRIGGERS

Triggers are stored programs, which are automatically executed or fired when some events occur. Triggers are, written to be executed in response to any of the following events:

- **database manipulation** statement (DELETE, INSERT, or UPDATE)
- **database definition** statement (CREATE, ALTER, or DROP).
- **database operation** (SERVER ERROR, LOGON, LOGOFF, STARTUP, or SHUTDOWN).

Triggers can be defined on the table, view, schema, or database with which the event is associated.

Benefits of Triggers:

- Triggers can be written for the following purposes "
- Generating some derived column values automatically
- Enforcing referential integrity
- Event logging and storing information on table access
- Auditing

- Synchronous replication of tables
- Imposing security authorizations
- Preventing invalid transactions

The general form of creating a trigger is:

```
CREATE [OR REPLACE ] TRIGGER trigger_name
{BEFORE | AFTER | INSTEAD OF }
{INSERT [OR] | UPDATE [OR] | DELETE}
[OF col_name]
ON table_name
[REFERENCING OLD AS o NEW AS n]
[FOR EACH ROW]
WHEN (condition)
DECLARE
Declaration-statements
BEGIN
Executable-statements
EXCEPTION
Exception-handling-statements
END;
```

Where,

- ✓ CREATE [OR REPLACE] TRIGGER trigger_name "Creates or replaces an existing trigger with the *trigger_name*.
- ✓ {BEFORE | AFTER | INSTEAD OF} "This specifies when the trigger will be executed. The INSTEAD OF clause is used for creating a trigger on a view.
- ✓ {INSERT [OR] | UPDATE [OR] | DELETE} "This specifies the DML operation.
- ✓ [OF col_name] "This specifies the column name that will be updated.
- ✓ [ON table_name] "This specifies the name of the table associated with the trigger.
- ✓ [REFERENCING OLD AS o NEW AS n] "This allows you to refer to new and old values for various DML statements, such as INSERT, UPDATE, and DELETE.
- ✓ [FOR EACH ROW] "This specifies a row-level trigger, i.e., the trigger will be executed for each row being affected. Otherwise, the trigger will execute just once when the SQL statement is executed, which is called a table-level trigger.
- ✓ WHEN (condition) "This provides a condition for rows for which the trigger would fire. This clause is valid only for row-level triggers.

Example:

Illustration of the trigger on employee table

```
CREATE OR REPLACE TRIGGER alert_salary_changes
BEFORE DELETE OR INSERT OR UPDATE ON employee
FOR EACH ROW
WHEN (NEW.ID > 0)
DECLARE
salary_diff number;
BEGIN
salary_diff := :NEW.salary - :OLD.salary;
dbms_output.put_line('Old salary: ' || :OLD.salary);
dbms_output.put_line('New salary: ' || :NEW.salary);
dbms_output.put_line('Salary difference: ' || salary_diff);
END;
```

UNIT SUMMARY

- **STRUCTURED QUERY LANGUAGE (SQL-99)**
- Glossary of basic SQL commands:
  - CREATE - creates a new table/view
  - INSERT - inserts new data into a database
  - SELECT - extracts data from a database
  - UPDATE - updates data in a database
  - DELETE - deletes data from a database
  - ALTER - modifies the schema or view
  - DROP - deletes a table
  - RENAME – rename a table
  - COMMIT – buffer to a disk
  - ROLLBACK – rollback the changes made
  - GRANT – Assign privileges to users
  - REVOKE – remove the assigned privileges
- **INTEGRITY CONSTRAINTS:**

The integrity constraints(IC) will protect the database from being accidentally damaged by ensuring that approved changes to the database do not cause a loss of data consistency.

- **Primary Key:** Is having the property of not null and unique.
- **Foreign key**: It establishes the relationship among tables.
- **Not null:** It does not allow a null value for that attribute.
- **DOMAIN CONSTRAINTS:**

Domain constraints can be created along with attribute specification or using create a domain. Once a new domain is created, then we can refer data type with the created domain name.

- **DATA TYPES IN SQL:**

The data types of SQL include numeric, character, bit, Boolean, date, and time.

Numerical data: The specific data types include smallint, int, numeric, real, and float.

String Data: The specific data types to handle fixed length strings include char and varchar data types.

CLOB (Character large objects): variable-length string data type. It is used to specify having large text values, such as documents.

Data and Time data: The specific data types to handle date and time includes the date, time, and timestamp.

Timestamp: It includes the DATE and TIME fields, along with a minimum of six decimal fractions of seconds and an optional WITH TIME ZONE qualifier.

Other types of data:

Bitstring: BIT(n) - A fixed length of a maximum number of bits n.

BLOB - BINARY LARGE OBJECT

It is a variable-length bitstring. It is used to store a large binary value such as images.

Boolean: In SQL, a tri value UNKNOWN, TRUE and FALSE.

- **ATTRIBUTE CONSTRAINTS AND DEFAULTS**

  NOT NULL constraint: SQL allows NULL values to the attributes.

  UNIQUE key constraint: Used to ensure that the information in the column for each record is unique. A table may have more than one unique key.

  DEFAULT clause: used to define a value as a default value to the attribute.

  CHECK clause: used to restrict the specified constraint and default values to the

SQL AGGREGATE OPERATORS

1. **Count**: It returns the count of a tuple in that column. If a DISTINCT keyword is used then it will return only the count of a unique tuple in the column. Otherwise, it will return a count of all the tuples (including duplicates) count (*) indicates all the tuples of the column.
2. **SUM**: It returns the sum of all the values in that column. If a DISTINCT keyword is used then it will return the sum of all unique values in the columns.
3. **AVG**: It returns the average value of that column values. If a DISTINCT keyword is used then it will return the average of distinct values only.
4. **MAX**: It returns the highest value of that column.
5. **MIN**: It returns the lowest value of that column.

SET OPERATIONS - SQL supports set operations over two relations to construct queries such as union, intersect, and except; IN /NOT IN and >some / > all.

Complex Queries:

Complex queries are not possible to write in a single SQL block. Two ways to compose a complex query in multiple SQL blocks.

Derived relations - SQL allows a sub-query expression to be used in the *from* clause.

With clause - provides a temporary view and is available in a query.

Aggregation with Groupingby using group by clause

- **VIEWS**

SQL view is a virtual table, which is dynamically constructed for a user-specific by extracting data from base table(s). operation on views are:

Create a view, updating a view, Selecting data from a view, and Dropping a view

- **SECURITY**

Assigning a user's privileges to parts of the database is called authorization. Authorizations on data may include, reading, inserting new data, updating data, and deleting data.

- **Granting or revoking**

SQL data definition language (DDL) provides a set of commands like grant, revoke to confer, and revoke privileges. The grant statement is used to confer authorization. To revoke an authorization, SQL provides a **revoke** keyword. SQL provides the privileges of selecting, inserting, updating, and deleting.

SQL PROGRAMMING TECHNIQUES - The PL/SQL programming language as a procedural extension language for SQL was developed by Oracle Corporation in the late 1980s available as an Oracle database.

STRUCTURE OF PL SQL BLOCK- PL/SQL programming units organize the code into blocks.

Declaration section - Used to define data types, structures, and variables. Declare variables by giving names, data types, and initial values.

Execution section -Used to place the code or logic in block structure and it must have at least one statement. Starts with BEGIN keyword.

Exception section - Used to handle exceptions through either catch or handle.

Named Block - A named Block is a type of block that starts with the header section which specifies the name and the type of the block. There are two types of blocks; Procedures and Functions

- **PL/SQL – OPERATORS**

The list of operators used in programming - Arithmetic operators, Relational operators, Comparison Operators, Logical Operators

- **SEQUENCES**

A sequence is an object in Oracle that is used to generate a number sequence. This can be useful when you need to create a unique number to act as a primary key.

Operations are: Create Sequence and DROP sequence

- **PL/SQL CONTROL STRUCTURES**

Testing Conditions: IF and CASE Statements. There are three forms of IF statements: IF-THEN, IF-THEN-ELSE, and IF-THEN-ELSIF

LOOP- END LOOP – control statement

EXIT-WHEN [EXIT– unconditionally stops the iterations. WHEN conditionally stop the loops.] and **FOR-LOOP**

- **CURSORS** - A **cursor** is a pointer to the context area. A cursor holds the rows (one or more) returned by a SQL statement. There are two types of cursors Implicit cursors and Explicit cursors
- **TRANSACTIONS** - A database **transaction** is an atomic unit of work that may consist of one or more related SQL statements.
- **PROCEDURES AND FUNCTIONS** - A subprogram is a program unit/ module that performs a specific task. PL/SQL subprograms are named PL/SQL blocks that can be invoked with a set of parameters. PL/SQL provides two kinds of subprograms

  Functions - return a single value; mainly used to compute and return a value.

  Procedures - do not return a value directly; mainly used to act.

- **EXCEPTIONS HANDLING** - System-defined exceptions and User-defined exceptions
- **TRIGGERS** - Triggers can be defined on the table, view, schema, or database with which the event is associated.

EXERCISES

Multiple Choice Questions

1 SQL stands for

a. semantic query language

b. stored query language

c. structured query language

d. self query language

2 ....commands are used to create a table, index, or view.

i. domain

j. create

k. DDL command

l. attribute

3 The .... supported by SQL are used to define domain constraints of attributes.

a. data types

b. integrity constraints

c. column names

d. key attributes

4 The attribute holding the values as not null and unique, then it is termed as .... key attribute

a. REFERENTIAL

b. NOT NULL constraint

c. NULL

d. PRIMARY

5 The table having more than one attribute as the primary key, then it is termed as.........

a. primary key

b. foreign key

c. composite key

d. referential key

6 In the usage of the foreign key, the attribute should possess the property of ....

a. primary key in referential table

b. not null in referential table

c. should possess same data type in both tables

d. ALL

7 The database system has several virtual schemas according to the level of ....

a. user interest

b. abstraction

c. concise view

d. none

8 .... keyword is used to specify a condition

a. where

b. group

c. IN

d. from

9 .... keyword is used to perform grouping.

a. where

b. group BY

c. IN

d. from

10 The .... is used to insert rows or add a new row of data into the existing table or view.

a. alter

b. insert

c. select

d. create

11 The drop table command is used to delete .... of the table

a. delete rows

b. delete schema

c. delete both

d. delete constraints

12 ________ are used to handle events on database with updations

a. procedures

b. functions

c. tiggers

d. sequences

13 ________ is used to generate the numbers in a pattern to maintain unique property of an attribute.

a. sequence

b. order

c. function

d. trigger

14 INOUT parameter indicates.........

i. Input string
j. Output string
k. Input and output same
l. takes an input value and returns the output value

Answers to MCQs:

1	2	3	4	5	6	7	8	9	10	11	12	13	14
C	B	A	D	C	D	B	A	B	B	C	C	A	D

Short and Long Answer Type Questions

1. Illustrate the basic structure of a SQL query.

2. List the basic SQL commands with examples used for creating and managing relations

3. Summarize the integrity constraints supported by SQL with examples

4. List SQL-supported set operations to perform join queries with specific examples.

5. Outline the comparison and logical operators supported by SQLwith specific examples.

6. Summarise the various security privileges of database.

7. Arrange the data (CSE, ECE, AERO, ME, IT) in chronological order to display the results.

8. Explain various clauses used to perform grouping, and aggregation available in SQL.

9. How to modify the structure of the table or change the constraints of the existing table.

10. Write a query to find the distinct customers and loan amounts of the branches situated in "Delhi" where the customers have taken the loans.

Numerical Problems

1. Build the subsequent queries in SQL, using the customer's schema.

a. List the offered products in the sore in electronics category items related to laptop.

b. List the customer names whose last name with Choudhary.

c. List the customers having income more than 60000.

2. Consider the employee database. Build queries using SQl and PL/SQL programming

a. Retrieve the employee names who are working for "DBS Bank" and staying in the city 'hyderabad'.

b. Create a sequence of customer numbers with a pattern of category name and sequence numbers. Example: ELEC001 starts for electronics category customers.

c. create a trigger to alert the updation in a salary and maintain a salary history table on each update.

PRACTICAL

1. A bank wants to automate each transaction. It provides the subsequent account types: Fixed Deposit (FD), Recurring Deposit (RD), and Savings Bank (SB)

The Bank also wants to monitor the loans granted to its clients. Create the relations with appropriate table names, attributes, datatypes and constraints.

Consider the following presumptions:

a. A customer is limited to having a single type of account. Joint accounts are not permitted

b. Only when a consumer has at least one of the account kinds is a loan available.

Use SQL for retrieving

a. account details of all fixed deposits

b. the account details of both fixed deposits and savings bank account

2. To represent the requirements of a small computer business corporation. Create, insert and retrieve the data by specifying domain constraints

Relation 1 - The company workers assemble several computer models. Each employee's employee number, name, address, phone number, job title, and salary.

Relation 2 - The model, specifications, name, and quantity of each machine.

Relational instance - Each machine is made up of various components. The parts that are on hand must be listed in an inventory. A record of each part's name, cost, and available quantity is kept.

Relation 3 - These components are purchased from a number of providers. The supplier's name, address, and phone number must be kept on file.

use SQL:

retrieve the computer details that have been assembled are sold.

Commercial DB systems:

- IBM DB2 - www.ibm.com/software/data/db2
- Oracle - www.oracle.com
- Microsoft SQL Server - www.microsoft.com/sql
- Sybase - www.sybase.com
- IBM Informix - www.ibm.com/software/data/informix

Free/public domain database systems:

- MySQL - www.mysql.com
- PostgreSQL - www.postgresql.org

REFERENCES AND SUGGESTED READINGS

- Henry F Korth, Abraham Silberschatz, “Database system concepts”, sixth ed., McGraw-Hill International editions, Computer Science Series
- Elmasri, Navathe, "Fundamentals of Database Systems", Elmasri, Navathe, Third ed, Addison Wesley
- Raghurama Krishnan, Johannes Gehrke, Database Management Systems, 3rd Edition, Tata McGraw Hill.
- C. J. Date, "An introduction to Database Systems", Sixth ed., Narosa Publications
- Database management systems- NPTEL: https://nptel.ac.in/Subjects/106105175

Dynamic QR Code for Further Reading
Structured Query Language

Data definition using SQL

Basic SQL query block and subqueries

Correlated subqueries

https://nptel.ac.in/Subjects/106106220

5 FUNCTIONAL DEPENDENCIES AND NORMALIZATION FOR

UNIT SPECIFICS

Through this unit we have discussed the following aspects:

- *Functional dependency in relational schemas*
- *Preserving database design quality with Normalization*
- *Database design algorithms*
- *Additional types of dependencies based on key constraint inclusions, Arithmetic Functions and Procedures*

The practical applications of the topics are discussed for generating further curiosity and creativity as well as to improve problem-solving capacity.

Besides giving a large number of multiple choice questions as well as questions of short and long answer types marked in two categories following lower and higher order of Bloom's taxonomy, assignments through several numerical problems, a list of references, and suggested readings are given in the unit so that one can go through them for practice. It is important to note that for getting more information on various topics of interest some QR codes have been provided in different sections which can be scanned for relevant supportive knowledge.

After the related practical, based on the content, there is a "Know More" section. This section has been carefully designed so that the supplementary information provided in this part becomes beneficial for the users of the book. This section mainly highlights the initial activity, examples of some interesting facts, analogy, history of the development of the subject focusing on the salient observations and finding, timelines starting from the development of the concerned topics up to the recent time, applications of the subject matter for our day-to-day real life or/and industrial applications on a variety of aspects, case study related to environmental, sustainability, social and ethical issues whichever applicable, and finally inquisitiveness and curiosity topics of the unit.

RATIONALE

The objective of relational database design is to develop a collection of relation schemas that allows us to store information without redundancy while allowing facilitates its retrieval. The relational database is made up of various schemas, each of which has a number of attributes. We had assumed up until this point that attributes are organized into relational groups using the database designer's common sense or by translating a conceptual data models like ER or enhanced-ER (EER) models, into a database schema design. Using these models the identification of entities, relationships, and associated attributes, and the mapping processes covered in Chapter 3 result in a logical combination of the attributes into relations. We still need a formal method, though; to examine the grouping of attributes into a relation schema could be preferable to another. In Chapters 3 focus on the database design, we did not create any appropriateness or goodness metrics to assess the design's quality outside of the designer's intuition. In this chapter, we go through some of the theory that has been created to assess the design quality of relational schemas, or to quantify why one set of attribute groupings into relation schemas is preferable to another. The quality of relational schemas can be discussed on two different levels. In the first, users' interpretations of relation schemas and the significance of their properties are expressed at a logical (or conceptual) level. Good relation schemas at this level allow users to accurately build their queries by helping them comprehend the meaning of the data in the relations. The second level refers to the physical storage (or implementation) of the base relation's tuples. The concept of identification of functional dependencies, a formal constraint among attributes that serve as the primary technique for formally evaluating the suitability of attribute groups into relation schemas, is the focus of this chapter. We talk about normal forms and how normalizing works by employing functional dependencies. A set of desirable constraints described by primary keys and functional dependencies are used to define successive normal forms. The normalization process entails conducting a succession of tests on relations to ensure that they satisfy these progressively demanding specifications and, when necessary, decomposing the relations. Discuss normal forms(from 1NF to 5NF) that can be used to analyze any design without the need for meticulous examination and normalization. Covers extended topics like multivalued dependency and join dependency.

Databases are an important branch of computer science that essentially deals with information and data and their effect on information retrieval. Database system implementation needs as a prerequisite step in data modeling and it is termed relational database management. This permits one to analyze the operations of many day-to-day transactions around us. Its practical applications are related to the model, construction, and operation of different types of database systems and tools.

PRE-REQUISITES

Mathematics: Calculus, Algebra (Class XII)
Computer Science: problem-solving with programming (Class XII)

UNIT OUTCOMES

Further dependencies

The List of outcomes of this unit is as follows:

U5-O1: Identify the functional dependencies in databases.

U5-O2: Summarize the various normal forms in the normalization of databases.

U5-O3: Make use of normal forms to remove the dependencies in databases

U5-O4: Outline the database design algorithms.

Unit-1Outcomes	EXPECTEDMAPPINGWITHCOURSEOUTCOMES (1-WeakCorrelation;2-Mediumcorrelation;3-StrongCorrelation)					
	CO-1	CO-2	CO-3	CO-4	CO-5	CO-6
U5-O1	2	2	3	-	-	-
U5-O2	2	2	2	-	-	-
U5-O3	3	3	3	-	-	-
U5-O4	3	3	3	-	-	-

5.1. DESIGN GUIDELINES FOR RELATIONAL SCHEMAS

The relational schema design quality is measured by using four informal guidelines:

- In the schema definition, the attribute semantics are clear
- Minimizing the data redundancy
- Minimizing the NULL value data
- Not allowing the chance of generating erroneous data tuple(s)

The guiding principle to design relational schema with good quality:

1. Create a relational schema that is simple to interpret. A single relation should not have properties from several entity types and relationship types. It makes sense intuitively that a relation schema's meaning can be easily explained if it corresponds to just one entity type or one type of relationship. Otherwise, semantic ambiguities may arise and the relationship will be difficult to understand if it refers to a combination of different entities and relationships.
2. Make that there are no insertion, deletion, or modification abnormalities when creating the base relation schemas. Construct the processes without any sort of anomalies while updating the database.
3. Avoiding attributes with NULL values in a base relation. If NULLs are inevitable, ensure that in exceptional cases and do not affect the majority of the tuples in the relation.
4. Create relational schemas joined on equality condition on correctly related attribute pairs (primary key, foreign key) in a way that ensures no erroneous tuple(s) are produced. Keep away from combining on relation schemas with matching attributes that aren't (foreign key, primary key) combinations, as doing so could result in erroneous tuples.

Example: A sample database named the Industry database was used. Information of employees, departments, and projects can be found in this database. A relational schema includes majorly:

- *Division: The Industry has numerous divisions. Each division is identified specifically by name, office location, and the person in charge of managing it.*
- *Project: A division has several projects, each with its own name, number, and budget.*
- *Employee(EMP) has a name, unique identification number, residence, wage, and birthdate. Although they are assigned to one division, employees might participate in many initiatives. Additionally, each employee's start date and immediate supervisor must be noted for each project.*
- *Dependent: Need to maintain each employee's dependents history with dependent_name, birthday, and relationship to the employee.*

Division

Div_No	Div_Name	Office location	Person in charge

Project

Proj_No	Proj_Name	Budget	Div_No

Employee_Member

Emp_No	Emp_Name	Residence location	wage	DOB

Fig. 5.1. Schema Diagram of Sample Industry Database

Division

Div_No	Div_Name	Office location	Person in charge_ID
01	sales	Delhi	1001

02	marketing	Bangalore	1008
03	establishment	Hyderabad	1019

Project

Proj_No	Proj_Name	Budget	Div_No
P1001	Sale charts management	200000	01
P1002	recruitment	300000	03
P1003	Promotions	800000	01
P1004	Salaries	600000	03
P1005	Customer attractions	500000	02

Employee_Member

Emp_No	Emp_Name	Residence location	wage	DOB
1001	Singh	Chhattisgarh	80000	1980-04-23
1002	Roi	Delhi	34000	1997-05-28
1003	Patel	Bangalore	59000	1990-09-26
1004	Nita	Delhi	57000	1987-02-01
1008	Aswin	Bangalore	90000	1978-06-21
1019	Vikas	Hyderabad	60000	1983-04-15

Employee-Project

Emp_No	Emp_Name	Proj_No	Proj_Name	months_worked
1001	Singh	P1001	Sale charts management	10
1002	Roi	P1002	recruitment	4
1003	Patel	P1001	Sale charts management	11
1001	Singh	P1004	Salaries	10
1008	Aswin	P1004	Salaries	12
1008	Aswin	P1005	Customer attractions	8

Fig. 5.2. Sample database state of Industry database

Fig. 5.2 explains a state of the schemas of industry database. The relational schema guidelines are accommodated in the design of database.

In the schema definition, the attribute semantics are clear - All these schemas are defined with clear semantics.

Minimising the redundant data in tuples – The goal of relational schema design is minimising the space of storage with minimal no. of attributes grouped to the relation. Storing join relation leads to the anomalies like insert, update and delete. Here all schemas grouped with appropriate set of attributes, so no chances of anomalies.

Minimising the NULL values in tuples – with NULL value attributes, many problems may rise like improper understanding on join operation, wastage of space, problem to perform aggregation operations (count, sum, average), when join and select on condition are performing, the results are unpredictable. All tuples are accommodated with relevant values. Hence no NULL value issue existed.

Not allowing the chance of generating erroneous tuples – While performing join on non key attribute tables, then leads to erroneous tuples. Here all tables are accommodated with primary key attribute. Hence no design issue existed.

5.2. FUNCTIONAL DEPENDENCY(FD)

A functional dependency (FD) is a tool to detect and analyse the design issues existed the schema design. It is a restriction between two or more sets of attributes in a database.

Definition: In a Relational schema, R= {C, C2, C3, ...Cn}; A functional dependency is denoted as C1 → C3, between two attributes C1 and C3 are subset of relation R specify that a check on possible tuples of a relation state r of R. Here condition is for any two tuples t1 and t3 in r have t1[C1] = t3[C1], they must have same t1[C3] = t3[C3].

This means the values of C3 components is dependent or determined by, the component C1.

C1 → C3 [termed as C1 implies C3] means functional dependency between C1 and C3; or in another way C3 is functionally dependent on C1

Example: Consider the relation schema Employee-Project shown in Fig. 5.2. from the semantics of the attributes and the relation, the functional dependencies identified are:

i. emp_no → Emp_name

ii. Proj_no → {Proj_name, Proj_location}

iii. { emp_no, Proj_no } → months_worked

The listed functional dependencies are identified due to...

(i) values of an employee's unique identification emp_id determines the employee's name (Emp_name),

(ii) values of a project's unique identification (Proj_no) determines the projectsname (proj_name) and the office_location (Proj_location),

(iii) values of a set emp_no, Proj_no determines the project working duration of the employee on currently associated project (months_worked).

5.3. NORMALIZATION OF RELATIONAL DATABASE SCHEMAS

The normalization of relations is analytical process through functional dependencies (FDs) and primary key to define the desirable properties of schema like minimising the redundancy and insertion, deletion and update anomalies. This is the process of making design have good quality using normal form test.

It provides to the DB designers:

1. A framework to analyze a relational schema based on their key constraints and the functional dependency existed among attributes.

2. A sequence of tests called normal forms that may be run on specific schemas to allow for any desired level of normalization of the relational database.

Normal form: Codd has proposed three normal forms, which are based on an mathematical (analytical) tool called functional dependency among the attributes of a relation. These are termed as first normal form(1NF), second normal form(2NF), and third normal form(3NF). Later Boyce and Codd were proposed with a strong definition of 3NF and termed as Boyce-Codd normal form (BCNF). Further two more normal forms are proposed as a fourth normal form (4NF) based on the multivalued dependencies and a fifth normal form(5NF) on join dependencies.

5.3.1. FIRST NORMAL FORM (1NF)

First normal form (1NF), which was designed to prevent attributes having values like multi-valued, composite, and their combinations, is the formal specification of a relation in the fundamental (flat) data model. It specifies that an attribute value must be atomic (means simple, and indivisible) and each tuple have a single value of same domain. As a result, 1NF prevents the attribute values from a set of multiple, a tuple, or a combination of both. The attribute values of single atomic (or indivisible) are permitted by 1NF.

Example: Consider the division schema shown in Fig. 5.3, whose primary key is Div_No, and Office locations attribute. Assume that each division is accommodated at multiple locations. The division schema sample state illustrates that not in 1NF since Office locations attribute value is not in an atomic state, as exemplified by the first and second tuples.

Office_locations attribute is having multi values, which is non aotomic. Hence, Normalization of division schema to keep in 1NF with multiple techniques:

- *By forming the primary key in the combination of {Div_No, Office_locations}; the drawback in this method is redundancy of data will create.*
- *If a max. no. of values (e.g.3) are known for the given attribute, then this attribute Office_locations is replaced by three atomic attribute names: Div_loc1, Div_loc2, and Div_loc3. The drawbacks of this method are*
  - *NULL values are allowed to non existing locations.*
  - *Expansion of locations leads to changes in structure of schema.*
  - *Ordering among locations is also difficult while querying.*

Division_schema

Div_No	Div_Name	Office_locations	Person in charge_ID

Sample state of Division

Div_No	Div_Name	Office_locations	Person in charge_ID
01	sales	{Delhi, Bangalore}	1001
02	marketing	{Delhi, Hyderabad, Bangalore}	1008
03	establishment	Delhi	1019

1NF form_division relation having redundancy

Div_No	Div_Name	Office_location	Person in_charge_ID
01	sales	Delhi	1001
01	sales	Bangalore	1001
02	marketing	Delhi	1008
02	marketing	Hyderabad	1008
02	marketing	Bangalore	1008
03	establishment	Delhi	1019

Fig. 5.3. Demonstration of Division relation Normalization into 1NF

5.3.2. SECOND NORMAL FORM (2NF)

Second normal form (2NF) is based on the concept of full functional dependency. A relation schema R is in 2NF if every nonprime attribute A in R is fully functionally dependent on the primary key of R. It is not partially dependent on any key of R.

> **Prime attribute vs non-prime attribute:**
> A prime attribute is member of candidate key in a relation schema R.
> A nonprime attribute is not a member of any candidate key in relation schema R.

> **Full functional dependency:**
> A FD, X → Y is a full functional dependency if removal of any attribute A from X means that the dependency does not hold anymore; i.e., any attribute A ∈ X, (X − {A}) does not functionally determine Y.

In Fig. 5.2; in the employee_project relation::

{emp_no, Proj_no} → months_worked is a full dependency

It holds emp_no → months_worked and Proj_no → months_worked

{emp_no, Pnumber} → Emp_Name is partial

It holds emp_no → Emp_Name.

> **Partial functional dependency:**
> A functional dependency X → Y is a partial dependency if some attribute A ∈ X can be removed from X and the dependency still holds; i.e, A ∈ X, (X − {A}) → Y.

Example: Consider the employee_project relation shown in Fig. 5.4. The tests for 2NF involve testing for functional dependencies (FD) whose left-hand side attributes are part of the primary key. (If a a single attribute primary key then the test not applicable.). It consists of 3 functional dependencies.

FD1: {emp_no, Proj_no} → months_worked

FD2: {emp_no} → emp_name

FD3: Proj_no → {Project_name, Proj_Location}

The employee_project relation is in 1NF but not in 2NF. Due to,

- *In FD2 the nonprime attribute Emp_name violates the 2NF because emp_name is functionally determined by emp_name.*
- *In FD3 the Proj_name and Proj_location are violating the 2NF test because Proj_name and Proj_location are functionally determined by Proj_no.*

***The solution to normalize into 2NF** is, it can be second normalized or 2NF normalized into a number of 2NF relations in which nonprime attributes are associated only with the part of the primary key on which they are fully functionally dependent. Hence the employee_project relation is **decomposed into 3 relations** named as Emp_Proj1, Emp_Proj2, and Emp_Proj3.*

Emp_Proj1: FD1: {emp_no, Proj_no} → months_worked

Emp_Proj2:FD2:Emp_no→ emp_name

Emp_Proj3:FD3: Proj_no → {Project_name, Proj_Location}

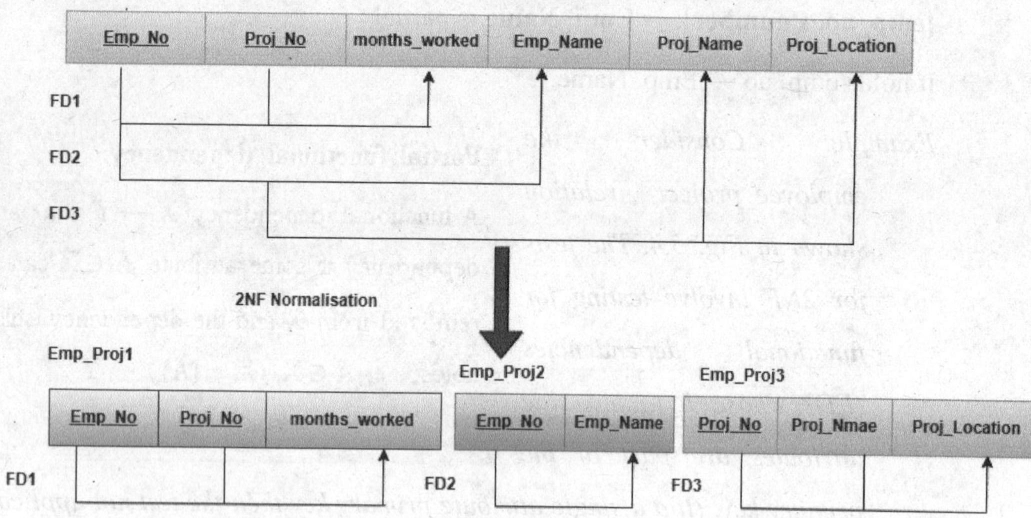

Fig. 5.4. Illustration of 2NF Normalization of Employee_project relation

5.3.3. THIRD NORMAL FORM (3NF)

Third normal form (3NF) is based on the concept of transitive dependency. A relation schema R is in 3NF if it satisfies 2NF and **no nonprime attribute of R is transitively dependent on the primary key.**

> Transitive dependency –
> A functional dependency $X \rightarrow Y$ in a relation schema R is a transitive dependency if there exists a set of attributes Z in R that is neither a candidate key nor a subset of any key of R, and both $X \rightarrow Z$ and $Z \rightarrow Y$ hold.

In 3NF - A nontrivial functional dependency $X \rightarrow A$ holds in R, either

(a) X is a superkey of R, or

(b) A is a prime attribute of R.

An Alternative Definition:

A relation schema R is in 3NF, if every nonprime attribute of R meets the following conditions:

- It is fully functionally dependent on every key of R.
- It is non transitively dependent on every key of R.

Example: Consider the employee_division relation shown in Fig. 5.5. The tests for 3NF involve testing for transitive dependencies whose nonprime attribute is transitively dependent on primary key. Here nonprime attribute personincharge_id is transitively derived from employee_id through Div_no.

The dependency emp_no → personincharge_id is transitive through div_name. It consists of 2 functional dependencies.

FD1: emp_no → {emp_name, DOB, Address, Div_no}

FD2: Div_no → {div_name, personincharge_id}

Emp_Division relation is in 2NF, since no partial dependencies on a key attribute exists. However, Emp_Division is not in 3NF because of the transitive dependency of personincharge_id (also div_name) on emp_no via Div_no. Hence, the solution to normalize to 3NF is Emp_Division relation is decomposing into two 3NF relation schemas Emp_div1 and Emp_div2. Though this the transitive dependency can be removed.

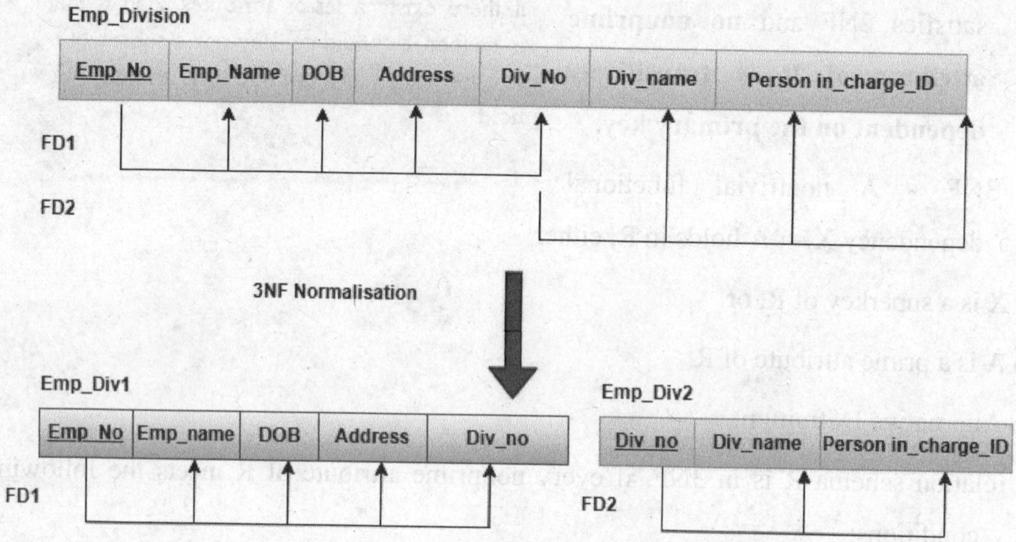

Fig. 5.5. Illustration of 3NF Normalization of Employee_division relation

Normal Form	Test	**Normalisation**
First Normal Form (1NF)	There should be no multivalued attributes or nested relations in a Relation.	Create new relations for each attribute with multiple values or nested relation.
Second Normal Form (2NF)	No nonkey attribute should be functionally dependent on a part of the primary key for relations whose primary key contains several attributes.	Decompose and establish a new relation for each partial key and dependent attribute (s). Maintain a relationship between the original primary key and any attributes that are functionally dependent on it.
Third Normal Form (3NF)	A nonkey attribute of a Relation should not be functionally determined by another nonkey attribute (or by a set of nonkey attributes). In other words, there should be no transitive relationship between a nonkey characteristic and the primary key.	Decompose and create a relation with the nonkey attribute(s) that functionally determine(s) the other nonkey attribute(s).

Fig. 5.6. Synopsis of various normal forms – Test to be performed – Normalization of schema of relations

5.3.4. BOYES CODD NORMAL FORM (BCNF)

Boyce-Codd normal form (BCNF) was proposed as a simpler form of 3NF, but it was found to be stricter than 3NF. That is, every relation in BCNF is also in 3NF; however, a relation in 3NF is not necessarily in BCNF.

Def. A relation schema R is in BCNF if whenever a nontrivial functional dependency X → A holds in R, then X is a superkey of R.

Differences of BCNF and 3NF definitions: The clause (b) of 3NF, which allow functional dependencies having the RHS as a prime attribute, is absent in BCNF. That makes BCNF a stronger normal form compared to 3NF.

Example: Consider a relation teaches shown in Fig. 5.6 with the following functional dependencies:

FD1: {Student, Course} → Instructor

FD2: Instructor → Course (with assumption of each instructor teaches one course)

The relation teaches is in 3NF but not satisfied the test of BCNF.

Hence, the solution to normalize to BCNF is teches relation is decomposing into two BCNF relation schemas teachs1 and teaches2. Though this, the nontrivial functional dependency is removed.

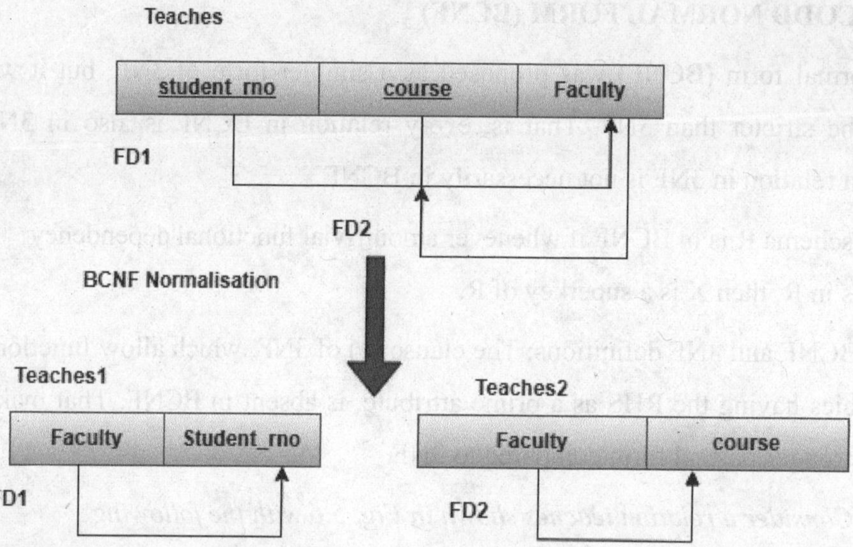

Fig. 5.7. Illustration of BCNF Normalization of teaches relation

5.3.5. FOURTH NORMAL FORM (4NF)

Fourth normal form (4NF) is based on the concept of multivalued dependency. A relation schema R is in 4NF with respect to a set of dependencies F (that includes functional dependencies and multivalued dependencies) if, for every nontrivial multivalued dependency X →→ Y in F+, X is a superkey for R.

> A multivalued dependency X → Y specified on relation schema R, where X and Y are both subsets of R, specifies the following constraint on any relation state r of R:
>
> If two tuples t1 and t2 exist in r such that t1[X] = t2[X], then two tuples t3 and t4 should also exist in r with the following properties,
>
> where we use Z to denote (R − (X ∪ Y)):
>
> t3[X] = t4[X] = t1[X] = t2[X]
>
> t3[Y] = t1[Y] and t4[Y] = t2[Y]
>
> t3[Z] = t2[Z] and t4[Z] = t1[Z]

Trivial MVD:::

An MVD X →→ Y in R is called a trivial MVD if

(a) Y is a subset of X, or

(b) X ∪ Y = R.

The test conditions should satisfy and normalization:

✓ The relation is always in BCNF while it has no FDs.

✓ A relation that is not in 4NF due to a nontrivial MVD must be decomposed to convert it into a set of relations in 4NF.

✓ The decomposition removes the redundancy caused by the MVD.

Example, Consider the relation employee_details in Fig. 5.7, consists of no FDs but has the MVD Emp_name →→ Proj_name | Dependent_name, hence the relation is not in 4NF. Hence, the solution to normalize to 4NF is employee_details relation is decomposing into two BCNF relation schemas Emp_Projects and emp_dependens. Though this, the non trivial multivalued functional dependencies are removed.

The trivial MVD in Emp_Projects relation

Emp_Name →→ Proj_name and

The trivial MVD in emp_dependens relation

Ename →→ Dname.

Employee_Member

Emp_Name	Proj_name	Dependent_name
Singh	Sale charts management	Jogi singh
Singh	recruitment	Lal Roi
Patel	Sale charts management	Veer patel
Aswin	Salaries	Neha
Aswin	Customer attractions	Neha

4NF Normalisation

Employee_Project

Emp_Name	Proj_name
Singh	Sale charts management
Singh	recruitment
Patel	Sale charts management
Aswin	Salaries
Aswin	Customer attractions

Employee_dependents

Emp_Name	Dependent_name
Singh	Jogi singh
Singh	Lal Roi
Patel	Veer patel
Aswin	Neha

Fig. 5.8. Illustration of 4NF Normalization of Employee_details relation

5.3.6. FIFTH NORMAL FORM (5NF)

Fourth normal form (5NF) is based on the concept of join dependency. A relation schema R is in fifth normal form (5NF) (or project-join normal form (PJNF)) with respect to a set F of functional, multivalued, and join dependencies if, for every nontrivial join dependency JD (R1, R2, … , Rn) in F+ (i.e, implied by F),every Ri is a superkey of R.

> **Join dependency (JD):**
> Denoted by JD (R1, R2, … , Rn) specified on relation schema R, specifies a constraint on the states r of R.
> The constraint states that every legal state r of R should have a non additive join decomposition into R1, R2, … , Rn.
> Hence, for every such r we have
> * (πR1(r), πR2(r), … , πRn(r)) = r
>
> – A join dependency JD (R1, R2, … , Rn), specified on relation schema R, is a trivial JD if one of the relation schemas Ri in JD (R1, R2, … , Rn) is equal to *R*.

Example, Consider the relation Product_supplies in Fig. 5.8, at any time a supplier_name s supplies a partner p, and a project j uses part p, and the supplier_name s supplies at least one part to project j, then supplier_name s will also be supplying part p to project j.

This constraint can be restated with a join dependency JD(R1, R2, R3) among the three projections R1 (supplier_name, Partner_name), R2 (supplier_name, Project_name), and R3 (Partner_name, Project_name) of SUPPLY.

Product_supply

Supplier_Name	Partner_name	Project_name
Singh	Jogi singh	Sale charts management
Singh	Lal Roi	recruitment
Patel	Veer patel	Sale charts management
Aswin	Neha	Salaries
Aswin	Neha	Customer attractions

5NF Normalisation

Relation1

Supplier_Name	Project_name
Singh	Sale charts management
Singh	recruitment
Patel	Sale charts management
Aswin	Salaries
Aswin	Customer attractions

Relation2

Supplier_Name	Partner_name
Singh	Jogi singh
Singh	Lal Roi
Patel	Veer patel
Aswin	Neha

Relation3

Partner_name	Project_name
Jogi singh	Sale charts management
Lal Roi	recruitment
Veer patel	Sale charts management
Neha	Salaries
Neha	Customer attractions

Fig. 5.9. Illustration of 5NF Normalization of Product supply relation

5.4. RELATIONAL DATABASE DESIGN ALGORITHMS

5.4.1. CLOSURE ALGORITHM

Algorithm 1: Determine A closure (A+) of functional dependency set F

Input: Set of Functional Dependencies (FDs)s called F on a relation schema R, and

a set of attributes A, is a subset of R.

A+ := A;

repeat

old A + := A +;

for each functional dependency Y → Z in F do

if A + □ Y then A + := A + ∪ Z;

until (A + = old A +);

5.4.2. MINIMAL COVER ALGORITHM

Algorithm 2: Finding a Minimal Cover F for a Set of Functional Dependencies E

Input: A set of functional dependencies E.

1. Set F := E.

2. Replace each functional dependency X → {A1, A2, … , An} in F by the n functional dependencies X →A1, X →A2, … , X → An. (*This places the FDs in a canonical form for subsequent testing*)

3. For each functional dependency X → A in F for each attribute B that is an element of X

   if { {F − {X → A} } ∪ { (X − {B}) → A} } is equivalent to F

   then replace X → A with (X − {B}) → A in F.

   (*This constitutes removal of an extraneous attribute B contained in the left hand side X of a functional dependency X → A when possible*)

4. For each remaining functional dependency X → A in F

   if {F − {X → A} } is equivalent to F,

   then remove X → A from F.

   (*This constitutes removal of a redundant functional dependency X → A from F when possible*)

5.4.3. FINDING KEY OF A RELATION

Algorithm 3: Finding a Key K for R Given a Set F of Functional Dependencies

Input: A relation R and a set of functional dependencies F on the attributes of R.

1. Set K := R.

2. For each attribute A in K

{compute (K − A)+ with respect to F;

if (K − A)+ contains all the attributes in R, then set K := K − {A} };

5.4.4. TESTING FOR NON ADDITIVE JOIN PROPERTY

Algorithm 4: Testing for Non additive Join Property

Input: A universal relation R, a decomposition D = {R1, R2, … , Rm} of R, and a set F of functional dependencies.

1. Create an initial matrix S with one row i for each relation Ri in D, and one column j for each attribute Aj in R.
2. Set S(i, j): = bij for all matrix entries. (*Each bij is a distinct symbol associated with indices (i, j)*)
3. For each row i representing relation schema Ri

{for each column j representing attribute Aj

{if (relation Ri includes attribute Aj) then set S(i, j): = aj;};}; (*Each aj is a distinct symbol associated with index (j)*)

4. Repeat the following loop until a complete loop execution results in no changes to S

{for each functional dependency X → Y in F

{for all rows in S that have the same symbols in the columns corresponding to attributes in X

{make the symbols in each column that correspond to an attribute in Y be the same in all these rows as follows: If any of the rows has an a symbol for the column, set the other rows to that same a symbol in the column. If no a symbol exists for the attribute in any of the rows, choose one of the b symbols that appears in one of the rows for the attribute and set the other rows to that same b symbol in the column ;} ; } ;};

5. If a row is made up entirely of a symbols, then the decomposition has the non additive join property; otherwise, it does not.

5.4.5. SYNTHESIS ON 3NF WITH DEPENDENCY PRESERVATION AND NONADDITIVE JOIN

Algorithm 5: Relational Synthesis into 3NF with Dependency Preservation and Nonadditive Join Property

Input: A universal relation R and a set of functional dependencies F on the attributes of R.

1. Find a minimal cover G for F (use Algorithm 15.2).
2. For each left-hand-side X of a functional dependency that appears in G, create a relation schema in D with attributes {X ∪ {A1} ∪ {A2} … ∪ {Ak} }, where X → A1, X → A2, … , X → Ak are the only dependencies in G with X as lefthand side (X is the key of this relation).
3. If none of the relation schemas in D contains a key of R, then create one more relation schema in D that contains attributes that form a key of R. (Algorithm 15.2(a) may be used to find a key.)
4. Eliminate redundant relations from the resulting set of relations in the relational database schema. A relation R is considered redundant if R is a projection of another relation S in the schema; alternately, R is subsumed by S.

5.4.6. DECOMPOSITION INTO BCNF WITH NONADDITIVE JOIN PROPERTY

Algorithm 6: Relational Decomposition into BCNF with Nonadditive Join Property

Input: A universal relation R and a set of functional dependencies F on the attributes of R.

1. Set D := {R} ;

2. While there is a relation schema Q in D that is not in BCNF do

{

choose a relation schema Q in D that is not in BCNF;

find a functional dependency X → Y in Q that violates BCNF;

replace Q in D by two relation schemas (Q − Y) and (X ∪ Y);

} ;

5.4.7. DECOMPOSITION INTO 4NF RELATIONS WITH NONADDITIVE JOIN PROPERTY

Algorithm 7: Relational Decomposition into 4NF Relations with Nonadditive Join Property

Input: A relation R and a set containing functional dependencies and multivalued dependencies F

1. Set D:= { R };
2. if A relational schema Q in D that is not in 4NF, do

{choose a relation schema Q in D that is not in 4NF;

find a nontrivial multi valued dependency: MVD X →→ Y in Q that violates 4NF;

replace Q in D by two relation schemas (Q − Y) and (X ∪ Y);

};

Algorithm	Purpose	Input	Output	Remarks
Algorithm 1	Determine all the attributes that can be functionally determined from *X*	An attribute or a set of attributes *X*, and a set of FDs *F*	A set of attributes in the closure of *X* with respect to *F*	The closure of a key is the entire relation
Algorithm 2	To determine the minimal cover of a set of dependencies F	A set of functional dependencies F	The minimal cover of functional dependencies	Multiple minimal covers may exist—depends on the order of selecting functional dependencies
Algorithm 3	To find a key K (that is a subset of R)	Relation schema R with a set of functional dependencies F	Key K of R	The entire relation R is always a default superkey
Algorithm 4	Testing for nonadditive join decomposition	A decomposition D of R and a set F of functional dependencies	Boolean result: yes or no for nonadditive join property	See a simpler test NJB in Section 14.5 for binary decompositions
Algorithm 5	Nonadditive join and dependency preserving decomposition	A relation R and a set of functional dependencies F	A set of relations in 3NF	BCNF, but achieves all desirable properties and 3NF
Algorithm 6	Nonadditive join decomposition	A relation R and a set of functional dependencies F	A set of relations in BCNF	No guarantee of dependency preservation
Algorithm 7	Nonadditive join decomposition	A relation R and a set of functional and multivalued dependencies	A set of relations in 4NF	No guarantee of dependency preservation

Fig. 5.10. Synopsis of Algorithms

5.5. FURTHER DEPENDENCIES

5.5.1. INCLUSION DEPENDENCIES

Inclusion dependencies were defined in order to formalize two types of inter relational constraints:

The foreign key (or referential integrity) constraint cannot be specified as a functional or multivalued dependency because it relates attributes across relations.

The constraint between two relations that represent a class/subclass relationship (see Chapters 4 and 9) also has no formal definition in terms of the functional, multivalued, and join dependencies.

Definition. An inclusion dependency R.X < S.Y between two sets of attributes - X of relation schema R, and Y of relation schema S - specifies the constraint that, at any specific time when r is a relation state of R and s is a relation state of S, we must have $\pi X(r(R)) \subseteq \pi Y(s(S))$

Here, it is not necessarily have to be a proper subset. Obviously, the sets of attributes on which the inclusion dependency is specified -X of R and Y of S - must have the same number of attributes. In addition, the domains for each pair of corresponding attributes should be compatible.

5.5.2. BASED ON ARITHMETIC FUNCTIONS AND PROCEDURES

The attributes of a relation may be related via some arithmetic function or a more complicated functional relationship. As long as a unique value of Y is associated with every X, we can still consider that the FD X → Y exists.

Example: ORDER_Record (Order#, Item#, Quantity, Unit_price, Extended_price, Discounted_price)

In this relation, (Quantity, Unit_price) → Extended_price

FD is existed by the formula Extended_price = Unit_price * Quantity

UNIT SUMMARY

- Informal Design Guidelines for Relational Schemas
- Functional Dependency (FD)
    - Full Functional Dependency
    - Partial Functional Dependency
    - Trivial Multi Value Dependency
- Normalization of relational database schemas
    - First normal form (1NF)
    - Second normal form (2NF)
    - Third normal form (3NF)
    - Boyes Codd normal form (BCNF)
    - Fourth normal form (4NF)
    - Fifth normal form (5NF)
- Relational database design algorithms
    - Closure Algorithm
    - Minimal cover algorithm
    - Finding Key of a relation
    - Testing for non-additive Join Property
    - Synthesis on 3NF with Dependency Preservation and Nonadditive Join
    - Decomposition into BCNF with Nonadditive Join Property
    - Decomposition into 4NF Relations with Nonadditive Join Property

Further dependencies based key properties and functions

- Inclusion Dependencies
- Based on Arithmetic Functions and Procedures

EXERCISES

Multiple Choice Questions

1 Identify a TRUE statement?

A. Every relation in 3NF is also in BCNF

B. A relation R is in 3NF if every non-prime attribute of R is fully functionally dependent on every key of R

C. Every relation in BCNF is also in 3NF

D. No relation can be in both BCNF and 3NF

2 Consider a relational table for student details with a single record for each registered student having the set of Attributes.

1. Roll_ Numer: Unique registration number of each admitted student

2. AADHAAR_Id: A Unique identity number, unique at the national level for each citizen

3. Bank Acc_ Number: Unique account number in the bank. A student can have multiple accounts or joint accounts. This attribute provisions the primary account number.

4. Name: Name of the student

5. Hostel_ Room: Room number of the hostel

Which one of the following option is INCORRECT?

A. Bank Acc_ Number is candidate key

B. Roll_ Number can be a primary key

C. AADHAAR_Id is candidate key if all students are from the same country

D. If S is a super key such that S∩ AADHAAR_Id is NULL then S∪ AADHAAR_Id is also a super key

3 The normal form which satisfies multi valued dependencies and which is in BCNF is

A. 4 NF

B. 3 NF

C. 2 NF

D. All of the mentioned

4 Consider the following relational schema:

Suppliers (sid: integer, sname: string, city: string, street: string)

Parts (pid: integer, pname: string, color: string)

Catalog(sid: integer, pid: integer, cost: real)

(sid, pid are primary keys)

Assume that, in the suppliers relation above, each supplier and each street within a city has a unique name, and (sname, city) forms a candidate key. No other functional dependencies are implied other than those implied by primary and candidate keys. Which one of the following is TRUE about the above schema?

A. The schema is in BCNF

B. The schema is in 3NF but not in BCNF

C. The schema is in 2NF but not in 3NF

D. The schema is not in 2NF

5 Consider the relation scheme R = {E, F, G, H, I, J, K, L, M, M} and the set of functional dependencies {{E, F} -> {G}, {F} -> {I, J}, {E, H} -> {K, L}, K -> {M}, L -> {N} on R. What is the key for R?

A. {E, F}

B. {E, F, H}

C. {E, F, H, K, L}

D. {E}

6 The maximum number of superkeys for the relation schema R(E,F,G,H) with E as the key is

A. 5

B. 6

C. 7

D. 8

7 Which one of the following statements about normal forms is FALSE?

A. BCNF is stricter than 3NF

B. Lossless, dependency-preserving decomposi-tion into 3NF is always possible

C. Lossless, dependency-preserving decomposi-tion into BCNF is always possible

D. Any relation with two attributes is in BCNF

8 In the __________ normal form, a composite attribute is converted to individual attributes.

A. First

B. Second

C. Third

D. Fourth

9 A table on the many side of a one to many or many to many relationship must:

A. Be in Second Normal Form (2NF)

B. Be in Third Normal Form (3NF)

C. Have a single attribute key

D. Have a composite key

10 Tables in second normal form (2NF):

A. Eliminate all hidden dependencies

B. Eliminate the possibility of a insertion anomalies

C. Have a composite key

D. Have all non key fields depend on the whole primary key

11 Which-one of the following statements about normal forms is FALSE?

A. BCNF is stricter than 3 NF

B. Lossless, dependency -preserving decomposition into 3 NF is always possible

C. Loss less, dependency – preserving decomposition into BCNF is always possible

D. Any relation with two attributes is BCNF

12 Functional Dependencies are the types of constraints that are based on______

A. Key

B. Key revisited

C. Superset key

D. None of the mentioned

13 Which is a bottom-up approach to database design that design by examining the relationship between attributes:

A. Functional dependency

B. Database modeling

C. Normalization

D. Decomposition

14 Which forms simplifies and ensures that there is minimal data aggregates and repetitive groups:

A. 1NF

B. 2NF

C. 3NF

D. All of the mentioned

15 Which forms has a relation that possesses data about an individual entity:

A. 2NF

B. 3NF

C. 4NF

D. 5NF

16 Which forms are based on the concept of functional dependency:

A. 1NF

B. 2NF

C. 3NF

D. 4NF

17 Empdt1(empcode, name, street, city, state,pincode).

For any pincode, there is only one city and state. Also, for given street, city and state, there is just one pincode. In normalization terms, empdt1 is a relation in

A. 1 NF only

B. 2 NF and hence also in 1 NF

C. 3NF and hence also in 2NF and 1NF

D. BCNF and hence also in 3NF, 2NF and 1NF

18 A property which ensures that each functional dependency is represented in some individual relational

A. Loss less join

B. Dependency preservation

C. Both [a] and [b]

D. None of the above

Answers to MCQs:

1	2	3	4	5	6	7	8	9	10	11	12	13	14	15	16	17	18
C	A	A	A	B	D	C	A	D	A	C	A	C	C	C	C	A	C

Short and Long Answer Type Questions

1. Define functional dependency? Why are some functional dependencies trivial?

2. Discuss normalization?

3. Illustrate functional dependency with example?

4. Differentiate fully functional dependency with partial functional dependency?

5. Demonstrate transitive dependency? Give an example?

6. Imagine creating a video portal that is similar to YouTube. Think of the data in a system for processing files. Describe how each of these elements relates to the storage of actual video data as well as to the information that describes the video, such as the title, the user who uploaded it, tags, and the users who watched it.

7. Illustrate a relational database design for a hospital management system with a set of patients and medical doctors. A patient log contains a history of tests conducted and consultations made.

8. Design a relational database for maintaining a track of the sports team based on interest. Then a system should store the matches played, the scores in each match, the players in each match and individual player statistics for each match. Summary statistics should be accommodated as derived attributes.

9. Summarise the different types of normal forms with significant examples.

10. Consider the following relational schemes for a library database:

Book (Title, Author, Catalog_no, Publisher, Year, Price)

Collection (Title, Author, Catalog_no)

the following are functional dependencies:

a. Title Author --> Catalog_no

b. Catalog_no --> Title Author Publisher Year

c. Publisher Title Year --> Price

d. Assume {Author, Title} is the key for both schemes. Apply the appropriate normal form for Book and Cancellation?

11. Outline the different types of dependencies other than functional.

12. Write an algorithm for decomposition into 4NF Relations with Nonadditive Join Property.

Numerical Problems

1.It has been determined by Amazon.com to rearrange its database. Books, sales, and user data are all stored. Amazon collects as much data as it can on user behaviour so that it can analyse it and make site improvements. Here are a few prerequisites:

(a) Each user is assigned a special ID, name, password, and email address. Amazon emails consumers on a regular basis, thus it's crucial to know if the user is okay with being spammed and if their email address has been returning messages.

(b) Amazon keeps track of a user's most recent visit date so that it can show the user a list of products that have been added to the site since his previous visit.

(c) Books are identified by their ISDN number, title, author, publisher, and 2. According to the above change, illustrate the schema diagram of restructured columns in the COURSE, SECTION, and PREREQUISITE relations so that only one column will need to be updated.

Design a relational database schema for the above-mentioned data,

PRACTICAL

1. A bank wants to automate each transaction. It provides the subsequent account types: Fixed Deposit (FD), Recurring Deposit (RD), and Savings Bank (SB)

The Bank also wants to monitor the loans granted to its clients. Determine the entities, their properties, and any relationships among them.

Design and create a relational schema using any open-source database systems (MySQL) and make sure to provide all explicit assumptions. Consider the following presumptions:

a. A customer is limited to having a single type of account. Joint accounts are not permitted.

b. Only when a consumer has at least one of the account kinds is a loan available.

2. To represent the requirements of a small computer business corporation, create an entity-relationship diagram:

a. The company's workers assemble several computer models. Each employee's employee number, name, address, phone number, job title, and salary are all kept on file.

b. The model, specifications, name, and quantity of each machine are also kept on file.

c. Each machine is made up of various components. The parts that are on hand must be listed in an inventory. A record of each part's name, cost, and available quantity is kept.

d. These components are purchased from a number of providers. The supplier's name, address, and phone number must be kept on file.

Computers that have been assembled are sold.

An effective Database design using Normalization

Consider the Insurance Plan Management System, a well-known and widespread issue in the modern world. For this issue, the Software Requirements Specifications (SRS) are as follows:

1. *The Insurance Provider includes numerous branches, each of which has a branchid, branch name, and/or address, location, contact information, fax, etc.*
2. *There are several staff members employed in each branch. For illustration, there is a manager, field agents, staff members who work in development, secretarial assistants, etc. It keeps track of staff members' names, addresses, positions, salaries, and dates of employment or birth.*
3. *In addition to full-time employees, there are part-time workers known as insurance agents who are commission-based employees.*
4. *The insurance provider is required to keep policyholder information on file. the policyholder address, tenure, maturity amount, policy number, and name*

With the knowledge of E-R diagrams studied so far, Identify the entity types, attributes related to entity and relationships.

KNOW MORE

Normal form illustration

https://www.geeksforgeeks.org/normal-forms-in-dbms/

REFERENCES AND SUGGESTED READINGS

- Henry F Korth, Abraham Silberschatz, “Database system concepts”, sixth ed., McGraw-Hill International editions, Computer Science Series
- Elmasri, Navathe,"Fundamentals of Database Systems", Elmasri, Navathe,Third ed, Addison Wesley
- Raghurama Krishnan, Johannes Gehrke, Database Management Systems, 3rd Edition, Tata McGraw Hill.
- C.J.Date, "An introduction to Database Systems", Sixth ed., Narosa Publications
- Database management systems- NPTEL: https://nptel.ac.in/courses/106105175

Dynamic QR Code for Further Reading

Further Reading about –Normalization in NPTEL

Topics discussed:

- Normalization theory
- 1NF
- 2NF
- 3NF
- BCNF
- 4NF
- 5NF

https://nptel.ac.in/courses/106104135

REFERENCES FOR FURTHER LEARNING

- Henry F Korth, Abraham Silberschatz, “Database system concepts”, sixth ed., McGraw-Hill International editions, Computer Science Series
- Elmasri, Navathe,"Fundamentals of Database Systems", Elmasri, Navathe,Third ed, Addison Wesley
- Raghurama Krishnan, Johannes Gehrke, Database Management Systems, 3rd Edition, Tata McGraw Hill.
- Database management systems- NPTEL: https://nptel.ac.in/courses/106105175
- *Learning and certification: https://www.geeksforgeeks.org/dbms/*
- *MySQL learning and practice: https://www.w3schools.com/mysql/mysql_rdbms.asp*

MySQL online compiler: https://onecompiler.com/mysql

CO AND PO ATTAINMENT TABLE

Course outcomes (COs) for this course can be mapped with the programme outcomes (POs) after the completion of the course and a correlation can be made for the attainment of POs to analyze the gap. After proper analysis of the gap in the attainment of POs necessary measures can be taken to overcome the gaps.

Table for CO and PO attainment

Course Outcomes	**Expected Mapping with Programme Outcomes (1- Weak Correlation; 2- Medium correlation; 3- Strong Correlation)**						
	PO-1	**PO-2**	**PO-3**	**PO-4**	**PO-5**	**PO-6**	**PO-7**
CO-1	3	3	3	3	1	1	3
CO-2	3	2	2	2	1	1	3
CO-3	3	3	3	3	1	1	3

The data filled in the above table can be used for gap analysis.

INDEX